PYTHON FOR BEGINNERS

AMZ PUBLISHING

TABLE OF CONTENTS

TABLE OF CONTENTS

TABLE OF CONTENTS

TABLE OF CONTENTS

WHY PYTHON?

Python is a multi-paradigm programming language that can be run on various platforms such as Windows, Linux, Mac, etc. It is compatible with multiple programming patterns like functional, object-oriented, procedural, or imperative programming.

The list of use cases in which Python can be employed is never-ending, from developing web-based applications to handling databases, solving mathematical problems, and developing state-of-the-art machine learning and deep learning algorithms Python is used everywhere.

Its readable syntax, which impersonates a general human language, is easily understood by newcomers and makes it different from most of the programming languages. That is one of the major reasons why it is preferred by freshmen who want to get started and try their hands at programming.

Python is considered an interpreted language because it is backed by an interpreter system, which makes it easier for a programmer to debug their programs. Bugs can get caught as soon as they are encountered during the execution of the program.

Python Features

Python is one of the modern-day programming languages that have a bagful of features. In this section, we will take a look at some of its notable features.

- **Ease of learning:** As compared to other programming languages, Python has an elegant syntax that is designed keeping in mind human readability, thus writing in such a manner that it can be easily understood by new learners.
- **Compact syntax:** Unlike with other languages like C, C++, Java, etc., programs written in Python are much shorter in terms of lines of code because of its compact syntax, which allows for the writing of complex expressions within a single line.
- **Open-source language:** It is licensed under the GNU General Public License (GPL) and is also approved by OSI and FSF, which makes it open-source and available for new contributions to the Python community.
- **Object-oriented programming:** Python supports most of the OOP concepts like Classes, Objects, Inheritance, Polymorphism, Abstraction, etc. However, Python is not fully object-oriented.
- **Interactive nature:** The chevron prompt (>>>) can be used for interactive programming in which a programmer can write and execute code directly on the terminal. It is useful in the case of the debugging of programs where bugs can be found easily.
- **Interpreted language:** Programs written in Python get executed via an interpreter, which makes it an interpreted language.
- **Dynamic nature:** Python supports dynamic typing that means a programmer need not declare the data type of each variable beforehand; it gets dynamically assigned at the runtime.

Python Features

- **Scalability:** Python has better environmental support for larger programs as compared to traditional shell scripting.
- **Portability:** Python programs can run on multiple platforms without making any explicit software changes. It supports all major OS like Windows, Linux, macOS, etc.
- **Extensibility:** Python modules are extendable in nature and custom functionality can be added to the existing modules to perform critical operations and maximize speed. We can even add custom functions to the Python interpreter.
- **Availability of vast library:** It comes with numerous built-in libraries and functions that can be used directly for performing tasks without any need for writing codes explicitly.
- **Dynamic memory allocation:** Inside Python, memory management is never an issue to any programmer. It comes with an implemented garbage collector that manages memory allocation and garbage collection on its own.

These are some features that Python possesses and that every Python programmer must know and understand. Several other features exist as well, which we will learn about later in this book as we proceed further with more specific topics.

An Appeal from the Publisher

Hello wonderful reader!

We hope you are enjoying this book.

We wanted to let you know that you have made an impact on many lives by reading this book.

Just to give you a brief introduction: We are a small publishing company with a team of 8 writers and 2 editors.

Most of our employees come from financially weaker section and our company is the only means they support their families. This is our way of giving back to the society.

We don't have the giant advertising budgets that many other publishers and businesses do online.

So, one way that you can really support our mission and our business is by leaving us a review on this book.

For a small company like us, getting reviews (especially on Amazon) means we can submit our books for advertising.

This means we can actually sell a few copies from time to time and make a bigger impact on the society as a whole. So, every review means a lot to us.

We can't THANK YOU enough for this!

GETTING PYTHON

In the last chapter, we learned that one of the key features of Python is its portability, which makes it suitable to run on multiple platforms and devices. Python supports all major operating systems such as Windows, Linux, Ubuntu, Solaris, CentOS, Mac OS, etc.

To write and run Python codes on our system, we must install Python first; later, we can write and execute codes. The Python community has an official website from where we can download and install the latest Python version onto our system. We can visit this website at https://www.python.org/downloads/.

When we visit the above-given link, we will be redirected to this website:

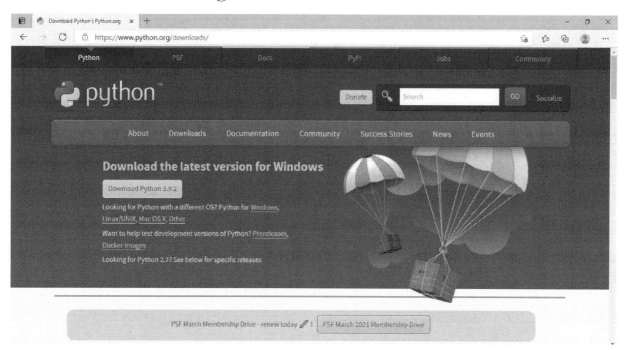

Installing Python

Installation on Windows

- If we want to install Python on a Windows machine, we must visit the official website at https://www.python.org/downloads/windows/ and look for the released versions of Python. We will then select whichever version we want to download from the available list. Here, we are going to download the currently released Python version 3.9.2

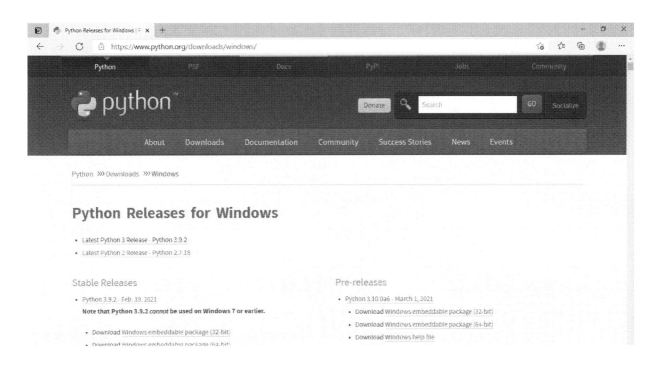

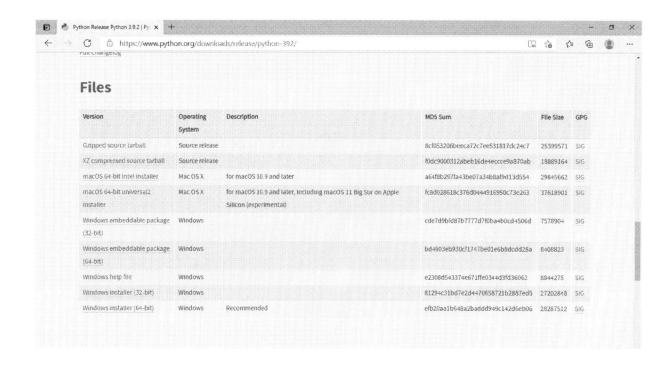

- When we click on the Python 3.9.2 link, we will be redirected to yet another page, where we can scroll down to see a list of compatible OS on which this Python version can be installed. From the list, we must select the Windows installer (32-bit/64-bit) depending on our system configuration.

Note: Here, we are selecting Windows installer (64-bit), as it matches the author's system requirements.

Files

Version	Operating System	Description	MD5 Sum	File Size	GPG
Gzipped source tarball	Source release		8cf053206beeca72c7ee531817dc24c7	25399571	SIG
XZ compressed source tarball	Source release		f0dc9000312abeb16de4eccce9a870ab	18889164	SIG
macOS 64-bit Intel installer	Mac OS X	for macOS 10.9 and later	a64f8b297fa43be07a34b8af9d13d554	29845662	SIG
macOS 64-bit universal2 installer	Mac OS X	for macOS 10.9 and later, including macOS 11 Big Sur on Apple Silicon (experimental)	fc8d028618c376d0444916950c73e263	37618901	SIG
Windows embeddable package (32-bit)	Windows		cde7d9bfd87b7777d7f0ba4b0cd4506d	7578904	SIG
Windows embeddable package (64-bit)	Windows		bd4903eb930cf1747be01e6b9dcdd28a	8408823	SIG
Windows help file	Windows		e2308d543374e671ffe0344d3fd36062	8844275	SIG
Windows installer (32-bit)	Windows		8129c31bd7e2d4470658721b2887ed5	27202848	SIG
Windows installer (64-bit)	Windows	Recommended	efb20aa1b648a2baddd949c142d6eb06	28287512	SIG

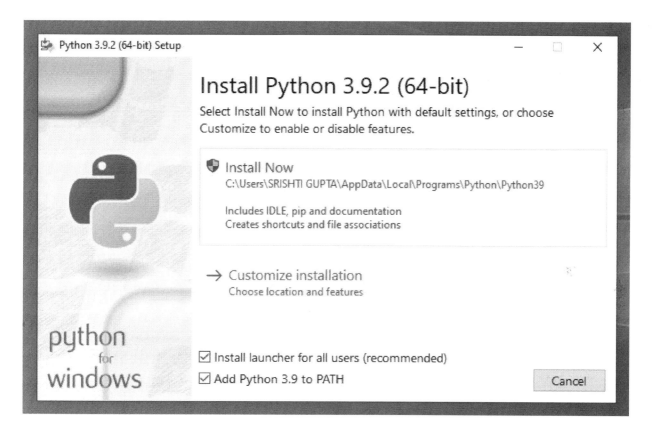

Upon selection, a .exe file, which is the installation wizard, will start downloading onto our system. Upon downloading, we must run the .exe installation wizard. An installation window will open as follows:

On the wizard, choose the default option, Install Now, and also click the checkbox given below to Add Python to PATH directly. The installer will run and Python will get installed on the system successfully.

Installation on Linux/Unix

- Nowadays, Python comes preinstalled on most Linux distributions. However, there can be cases in which certain features might not be available with the preinstalled version. In that case, we can easily update the old Python version from the source.
- There may also be cases in which Python is not preinstalled on your system. For this purpose, the Python organization provides us with dedicated documentation to set up Python on our system. This documentation can be found at:
  https://docs.python.org/3/using/unix.html

Installation on Mac OS

- To install Python on the Mac OS, we can visit the website https://www.python.org/downloads/mac-osx/. Just like we installed Python on Windows, we can install Python on Mac OS as well. For this, we can download the Python package file compatible with our Mac system; then we can run the installation wizard and install Python on our system.

Installation on other platforms

- To install Python on other platforms, simply visit https://www.python.org/download/other/ and look for other platforms on which Python can be installed.

Note: The official website provides documentation support that can be used to easily install Python.

Setting Path

Our program and executable files can exist in different directories, so the OS provides us with a suitable path where we can add the directories in which the OS searches for executable files for executing the Python commands. The path is stored inside the environment variable and we can add/edit this path to set up Python to run our Python files.

Adding Python on Windows Path

- One of the easiest ways to add Python to Windows PATH is by clicking the checkbox in the installation wizard (as was discussed above). However, sometimes, we want to add Python to the PATH manually. To do this, we must follow a series of steps:
    1. Press Windows + R command on your system to open the Run dialog box.
    2. In the Run dialog box, type the command 'sysdm.cpl' and hit OK to open the System Properties window.

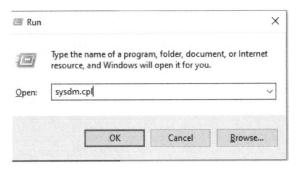

3. In the System Properties window, navigate to the Advanced tab. There, we can see an Environment Variables button at the bottom.

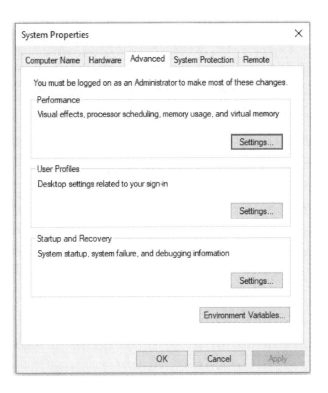

4. Click on the Environment Variables button to open a window. Here, we can set the new path or edit the existing path if not already given. We're not going to set up the path explicitly, as we already did this while installing Python using the installation wizard.

We can also add a Python directory to the path for a specific period as per our requirement. This can be done by executing the following command on the command line interface:

path %path%;C:\Python

It should be noted that C:\Python is the name of the directory that we want to add to the path. Here, the user can pass their own directory which they must add.

Below is a list of some important Python environment variables that are worth knowing:

Variable Name	Description
PYTHONPATH	This variable's function is similar to the PATH. It tells the interpreter where to look for module files that are written inside the program. Often, it is already preset by the installer. This variable should include the Python source library directory and also all the directories containing the Python source code.
PYTHONCASEOK	This variable is used in Windows OS to instruct Python to locate the first case-insensitive match in an import statement. We can set this variable to any value to activate it.
PYTHONHOME	This variable usually remains embedded inside the PYTHONSTARTUP or PYTHONPATH directories. It aids in switching module libraries easily.
PYTHONSTARTUP	This variable is executed every time we start the interpreter. The variable contains the path of an initialization file with the Python source code. Inside a UNIX-based OS, it exists with name .pythonrc.py and generally contains commands that are used either to modify PYTHONPATH or to load utilities.

Adding path on UNIX/LINUX

When we want to add a Python directory to the UNIX/LINUX path for a particular session, we can execute these commands:
In the csh cell, type the command:

setenv PATH "$PATH:/usr/local/bin/python"
and then hit the enter key on our keyboard to run the command.

In the bash shell (in Linux), type the command:
export ATH="$PATH:/usr/local/bin/python"

and then hit the enter key on our keyboard to run the command.
In the sh or ksh shell, type the command:
PATH="$PATH:/usr/local/bin/python"

and then hit the enter key on our keyboard to run the command.
The point that should be kept in mind is that /usr/local/bin/python is
the default path of the Python directory in all cases.

Running Python

When Python gets successfully installed on our system, we can run Python commands in three different ways:

Through the interactive interpreter

1. We can use the command line available in our system to write and execute Python commands interactively.

    For this, we must first start the command line and execute the first command as Python on the system. This will start the Python interpreter. Then we will see a chevron (>>>) symbol. On this chevron prompt, we can run our Python commands.

```
Command Prompt - Python                                        —    □    ✕
Microsoft Windows [Version 10.0.18363.1379]
(c) 2019 Microsoft Corporation. All rights reserved.

C:\Users\SRISHTI GUPTA>Python
Python 3.9.2 (tags/v3.9.2:1a79785, Feb 19 2021, 13:44:55) [MSC v.1928 64 bit (AMD64)] on win32
Type "help", "copyright", "credits" or "license" for more information.
>>>
```

2. Running a Python script on the command line

We can also run a Python script from the command line. To execute a Python script, we must save the script file with a .py extension. Then we can invoke the interpreter to execute the script.

Suppose we want to run a script named 'xyz'. Then we will save it with the name xyz.py. We can run it on the command line using the command as shown in the figure below:

If you did not have a clear understanding of this, do not worry, as you will get a fair idea about it in the upcoming chapters.

3. Running Python via an Integrated Development Environment (IDLE)

When we install Python on our system, it also installs an IDLE shell on which we can execute Python commands as well. We can run the Python IDLE and it will open a GUI editor in which we can write our code. Upon running, it will look like:

Note: Later in this book, we will be making heavy use of the Python IDLE for running our Python commands directly through interactive chevron or by writing scripts through it.

LEARNING PYTHON

Up to now, we have learned how we can set up our device to run Python programs over it. In this chapter, we will start our journey in the Python language by taking initial baby steps, writing our first Python code, and executing it.

Then we will increase our understanding of basic data types used inside the Python environment and how we can take inputs from the user.

Running Python

Writing the first piece of code and executing it successfully always gives a boost to one's confidence and sense of pride. I hope that you all are excited to write and execute your first Python program, as it will mark your first big step toward the world of programming in Python.

To start with, we will proceed with the most famous programming example: printing the 'Hello World!!' statement. Note that for the sake of simplicity, we will be writing the code on the IDLE that we installed earlier in the interactive mode using the chevron prompt.

To print the statement, we just need to use the print() method. We will pass the string that we want to print inside the method and then we will hit the Enter button. That's it. Congratulations!

We have just executed our first Python program. The string 'Hello World!!' will get printed out as the output onto the console.

```
IDLE Shell 3.9.2                                            —    □    ×
File  Edit  Shell  Debug  Options  Window  Help
Python 3.9.2 (tags/v3.9.2:1a79785, Feb 19 2021, 13:44:55) [MSC v.1928 64 bit (AM
D64)] on win32
Type "help", "copyright", "credits" or "license()" for more information.
>>>
>>> print('Hello World!!')
Hello World!!
>>> |
```

Variables

To store data, we require containers. We then need to reserve a certain amount of memory where we can store this data for processing. Python offers this container in the form of variables that can be used for storing data. We can think of a variable as a name given to an object. Using it, we can refer to that object inside the program environment whenever we want.

The variables can hold data of any type— a number, a string, floating numbers, Boolean values, or characters. We will be learning about these data types in the following section.

Assigning Values to Variables

To assign values to a variable, we use the assignment operator (=). As we discussed in chapter 1, one of the notable features of Python is that it is dynamically typed.

Thus, to assign values to a variable, we do not need to specifically declare the variables beforehand with a data type (as must be done in other programming languages like C, C++, Java, etc.). The data type of the variable gets automatically decided at runtime by the interpreter during execution. This could be done as:

```
>>> variable_1 = 123
>>> print(type(variable_1))
<class 'int'>
>>>
>>>
>>> variable_2 = 150.44
>>> print(type(variable_2))
<class 'float'>
>>>
>>>
>>> variable_3 = True
>>> print(type(variable_3))
<class 'bool'>
>>>
```

Note: We can use the **type()** function to identify the data type of a variable. As can be seen from the output of the print() statement in each case, the class to which those variables belong gets printed.

Multiple Variable Assignments

Python also provides us with an interesting feature that we can use to assign values to multiple variables in a single statement. This feature is not available in many programming languages.

```
>>>
>>> a,b = 'Hello','World'
>>> print(a)
Hello
>>> print(b)
World
>>> num1,num2,num3 = 10,20,30
>>> print(num1,num2,num3)
10 20 30
>>>
```

Data Types

Now that we know that variables can be used to store data items, we must learn about what kinds of data they can store. Python supports data in multiple forms, and the data belongs to a certain class. We know that Python is an object-oriented language and that each data type is actually a class. The variables that we use to store data are the instances/objects of those classes.

Following are some of the most commonly used data types in Python:

String

Strings are continuous sequences of character data enclosed within single or double quotation marks. The data enclosed inside the pair of opening and closing quotation marks is part of the string. The data type is represented under the **str** class.

Representation of Strings

Single-line strings

- As discussed, single-line strings can be represented by putting data inside the single and double quotation blocks. We can assign string values to the variables and then reference these strings using the variable names. Also, we can use the type() method to

verify the data type of the variables, as can be seen in the following example:

```
>>> var_1 = 'Hello'
>>> print(var_1)
Hello
>>> print(type(var_1))
<class 'str'>
>>>
>>>
>>> var_2 = "World"
>>> print(var_2)
World
>>> print(type(var_2))
<class 'str'>
>>>
```

- **Multi-line strings**

  To assign a variable multi-line string, we must enclose it inside triple single quotes. This can be done and verified as seen in the following example:

```
>>> var_3 = '''This is
a multi-line
string'''
>>> print(var_3)
This is
a multi-line
string
>>> print(type(var_3))
<class 'str'>
>>> |
```

Numeric

The numeric data type in Python can be used for storing numerical data that is present in the form of integers, floating values, complex numbers, etc. Python offers support for all this numeric data. There are four different classes in which we can divide the numeric data. These are:

Integers: Integers are stored inside the *int* class.

Long integers: Integers with very large values are kept under the *long* class.

Float: Floating point numbers/real values belong to the *float* class.

Complex numbers: Python also offers us the ability to use complex numbers, which are stored inside the *complex* class.

```
>>> num1 = 1234
>>> print(type(num1))
<class 'int'>
>>>
>>> num2 = 12.34
>>> print(type(num2))
<class 'float'>
>>>
>>>
>>> num3 = 10 + 20j
>>> print(type(num3))
<class 'complex'>
>>> |
```

Boolean

The Boolean data type gives us the ability to use True and False values. They are covered under the **bool** class. Any non-zero value can be thought of as a True value, whereas False is represented by zero.

```
>>>
>>> bool_1 = True
>>> print(type(bool_1))
<class 'bool'>
>>>
>>> bool_2 = False
>>> print(type(bool_2))
<class 'bool'>
>>>
>>>
```

List

Lists are one of the sequence data types that can be used to store data of multiple data types. Items in the list are stored inside square brackets ([]) and are separated from each other by commas (,). Lists can be compared with arrays that are available in other programming languages. Lists are mutable and offer us multiple methods to manipulate data. We will be learning more about lists and their functions separately in a different chapter.

```
>>>
>>> list_1 = ['Ram', 'a', 120, True, 12.22]
>>>
>>> print(type(list_1))
<class 'list'>
>>>
```

Data Type Conversion

When we are writing a piece of code, there are certain cases in which we need to change the data type of a variable. For those explicit cases, Python provides us with a range of handy functions that can be used to change the data type. Some of the functions are noted below in the table:

Function	Description
int()	int(z), it converts the z object to an integer.
float()	float(z), it converts the z object to a floating real value.
long()	long(z), it converts the z object to the long type value.
complex()	complex(z), it converts the z object to the complex number type value.
str()	str(z), it is used to convert an object to string type.
eval()	eval(str), when we pass a string object as a parameter, it evaluates the string and returns an object.
chr()	chr(z), it converts an integer z into a character type.
unichr()	unichr(z), it converts an integer z into Unicode character type.
ord()	ord(z), it returns the unicode equivalent of the corresponding z character.

User Input Values

Now that we have a basic idea about the data types that are used in Python, we will learn how to ask users to input data inside the program. For this purpose, we will be using the input() method. In this part, we will be writing the code inside a script. Then we will execute that script with the help of the command line. This will give you an idea about how to write a Python script and execute it with a command prompt.

We will start by writing the script inside a text file. You are free to use any text editor of your choice. Here, for explanation purposes, we are writing the script with the help of the Notepad text editor available in Windows OS.

```
File  Edit  Format  View  Help
name = input("Enter your name: ")
print("Your name is: ",name)
```

We will then save this script with the name of the form 'file_name.py'. Use of the .py extension to save the file is necessary because it signifies that it is a Python script.

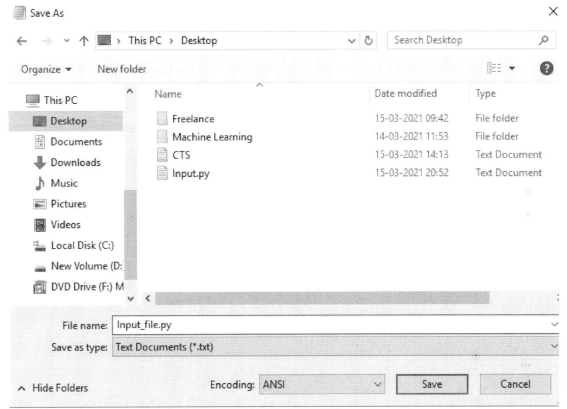

Note that the file is being saved on the Desktop having file name 'Input_file.py'. After saving the file, we will move to the command line and change our current working directory to the Desktop because our script is present at that location. Now, we will call the Python interpreter to execute this script. This can be done using the following command:

Python filename.py

When we run the command, the script will get executed. The input() method will halt for a moment and ask the user to enter the data.

```
Command Prompt - Python Input_file.py

Microsoft Windows [Version 10.0.15063]
(c) 2017 Microsoft Corporation. All rights reserved.

C:\Users\Saurabh Gupta>cd Desktop

C:\Users\Saurabh Gupta\Desktop>Python Input_file.py
Enter your name: _
```

When we enter the data and hit enter, the next line in the program will get executed and the print() statement will print the name using the name variable.

```
Command Prompt

Microsoft Windows [Version 10.0.15063]
(c) 2017 Microsoft Corporation. All rights reserved.

C:\Users\Saurabh Gupta>cd Desktop

C:\Users\Saurabh Gupta\Desktop>Python Input_file.py
Enter your name: Saurabh Gupta
Your name is:   Saurabh Gupta

C:\Users\Saurabh Gupta\Desktop>_
```

Note: It is mandatory to change the directory to the location where our file is located to run the script. Otherwise, our Python command will never find the script file and it will return a traceback error.

TYPES OF OPERATORS

In the previous chapter, you learned to write your first Python program. Then we discussed various data types that are available in Python. We also saw a Python program to read input values from the user. Having done all these things, we are now ready to proceed with learning new concepts. This chapter will increase your understanding of operators in Python and how and where they can be used.

Operators in Python are special symbols used to perform some operations over variables and values. The values over which these operators perform any operations are called operands. These are generally used to carry out some calculations but there are many other use cases, which we will see in the latter part of the chapter.

For example, 1 + 2 = 3; here, 1 and 2 are the numerical values and are known as the operands. The '+' and '=' symbols are the operators that are used to perform a certain operation over the operands. Here, the + operator performs the addition operation.

Arithmetic

The operators that are used to perform mathematical operations on numerical operands are called arithmetic operators. The different numerical operations are addition, subtraction, multiplication, division, exponentiation, etc. Below is a table consisting of different arithmetic operators along with their descriptions and syntax.

Operator Name	Description	Syntax
+ (Addition)	This is a kind of binary operator and requires two operands on either side of the operator. It sums the values of both the operands.	x + y
- (Subtraction)	This is also a binary operator and returns the difference of both the operands present on either side.	x − y
* (Multiplication)	This is also a binary operator and returns the product of both the operands present on either side.	x * y
/ (Division)	This is also a binary operator and returns the quotient value when the left-hand operand gets divided by the right-hand operand. The value is returned in the floating-point.	x / y
// (Floor Division)	This is just like the division operator but instead, it returns a floor value of the quotient.	x // y
% (Modulus)	This is also a binary operator and returns the remainder value when the left-hand operand gets divided by the right-hand operand.	x % y
** (Exponential/Power)	This is also a binary operator and returns the exponentiation value where the left operand is raised to the power of the right operand.	x **y

Let's learn more about this through hands-on practice. Up to now, we have executed our Python programs in two ways: first, via an interactive chevron prompt on the IDLE platform and second, via writing a Python script with the help of a text editor and then running it on the command line.

For this example, we will be using only our IDLE to write a Python script and then executing the script on the IDLE itself.
For this, you must open the IDLE on your PC and run it. If you observe the IDLE, you will notice a File option in the menu bar at the top. Click this File option and from the drop-down menu select the New File option. This will open up a text editor dialog box. We can use this text editor to write our scripts as in the image below:

```
Operators.py - C:\Users\Saurabh Gupta\AppData\Local\Programs\Python\Python39\Operators.py (3.9.2)     —   □   ×
File  Edit  Format  Run  Options  Window  Help

x = 10
y = 5

print("The value after addition is: ",x+y)

print("The value after subtraction is: ",x-y)

print("The value after multiplication is: ",x*y)

print("The value after division is: ",x/y)

print("The value after floor division is: ",x//y)

print("The modulus value after division is: ",x%y)

print("The remainder value after division is: ",x**y)
```

After writing the script, we must save the script, so we will press Ctrl + S to save it manually with the .py extension. After saving the file, we can execute this script directly from the IDLE by pressing the F5 shortcut key or via the Run option in the menu bar. This will run execute our script in the IDLE and the output will be shown as:

```
IDLE Shell 3.9.2                                              —  □  ×
File  Edit  Shell  Debug  Options  Window  Help
Python 3.9.2 (tags/v3.9.2:1a79785, Feb 19 2021, 13:44:55) [MSC v.1928 64 bit (AM
D64)] on win32
Type "help", "copyright", "credits" or "license()" for more information.
>>>
= RESTART: C:\Users\Saurabh Gupta\AppData\Local\Programs\Python\Python39\Operato
rs.py
The value after addition is:  15
The value after subtraction is:  5
The value after multiplication is:  50
The value after division is:  2.0
The value after floor division is:  2
The modulus value after division is:  0
The remainder value after division is:  100000
>>>
```

We can observe the output of the script and notice the working of the arithmetic operators.

Comparison (Relational)

These operators are used to compare values that are present on either side of the operator and return either a True or False value depending on the situation. These are also sometimes known as the relational operators, as they can be used to determine the relationship between the operands. Given below is a table consisting of different comparison/relational operators along with their descriptions and syntax.

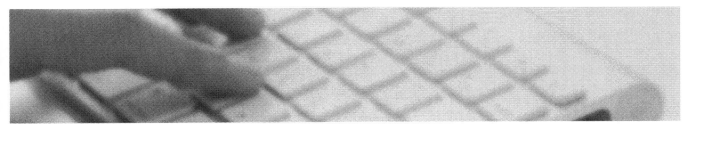

Operator	Description	Syntax
> (Greater than)	It returns a True value when the value of the left operand becomes greater than the right operand, otherwise False.	a > b
< (Lesser than)	It returns a True value when the value of the left operand becomes lesser than the right operand, otherwise False.	a < b
>= (Greater than or equal to)	It returns a True value when the value of the left operand becomes greater than or equal to the right operand, otherwise False.	a >= b
<= (Lesser than or equal to)	It returns a True value when the value of the left operand becomes lesser than or equal to the right operand, otherwise False.	a <= b
== (Equals to)	It returns a True value when the value of the left operand becomes equal to the value of the right operand, otherwise False.	a == b
!= (Not equals to)	It returns a True value when the value of the left operand remains not equal to the value of the right operand, otherwise False.	a != b
<> (Not equals to)	It returns a True value when the value of the left operand remains not equal to the value of the right operand, otherwise False.	a <> b

Let's learn more about this using an example.

```
*Operators.py - C:\Users\Saurabh Gupta\AppData\Local\Programs\Python\Python39\Operators.py (3.9.2)*          —   □   ×
File  Edit  Format  Run  Options  Window  Help
x = 10
y = 5
z = 10

print("Is x greater than y?: ",x>y)

print("Is x lesser than y?: ",x<y)

print("Is x greater than or equals to z?: ",x>=z)

print("Is x lesser than or equals to z?: ",x<=z)

print("Is x equals to z?: ",x==z)

print("Is x equals to y?: ",x==y)

print("Is x not equals to y?: ",x!=y)

print("Is x not equals to z?: ",x!=z)
```

When we execute the script, the output will be shown as:

```
= RESTART: C:\Users\Saurabh Gupta\AppData\Local\Programs\Python\Python39\Operato
rs.py
Is x greater than y?:  True
Is x lesser than y?:  False
Is x greater than or equals to z?:  True
Is x lesser than or equals to z?:  True
Is x equals to z?:  True
Is x equals to y?:  False
Is x not equals to y?:  True
Is x not equals to z?:  False
>>>
```

Assignment

These operators are used for assigning values to the variables. We use the (=) symbol for assigning the values present on the right-hand side of the operator to the variables present on the left-hand side of the operator.

Let's look at an example.

```
Operators.py - C:\Users\Saurabh Gupta\AppData\Local\Programs\Python\Python39\Operators.py (3.9.2)     —    □    ×
File  Edit  Format  Run  Options  Window  Help
x = 10
y = 5

print("The value assigned to x variable is: ",x)

print("The value assigned to y variable is: ",y)
```

When we execute the script, the output will be shown as:

```
= RESTART: C:\Users\Saurabh Gupta\AppData\Local\Programs\Python\Python39\Operato
rs.py
The value assigned to x variable is:   10
The value assigned to y variable is:   5
>>>
```

Augmented Assignment Operators

Augmented assignment operators are clubbed with few other operators to first perform designated operations and later assign the resultant values to the variables.

These are listed in the table below

Operator	Syntax	Syntax Equivalence
+=	x += y	x = x + y
-=	x -= y	x = x - y
*=	x *= y	x = x * y
/=	x /= y	x = x / y
//=	x //= y	x = x // y
%=	x %= y	x = x % y
**=	x **= y	x = x ** y

```
Operators.py - C:\Users\Saurabh Gupta\AppData\Local\Programs\Python\Python39\Operators.py (3.9.2)      —    □    ×
File  Edit  Format  Run  Options  Window  Help
x = 100
y = 50

print("Present value of x is: ",x)

print("Present value of y is: ",y)

x += y

print("The value of x after performing x += y is: ",x)

x -= y
print("The value of x after performing x -= y is: ",x)

x *= y
print("The value of x after performing x *= y is: ",x)

x /= y
print("The value of x after performing x /= y is: ",x)

|
```

After we execute the script, its output will be shown as:

```
>>>
= RESTART: C:\Users\Saurabh Gupta\AppData\Local\Programs\Python\Python39\Operato
rs.py
Present value of x is:  100
Present value of y is:  50
The value of x after performing x += y is:  150
The value of x after performing x -= y is:  100
The value of x after performing x *= y is:  5000
The value of x after performing x /= y is:  100.0
>>>
```

Here, suppose we have x = 100 and y = 50. Then,
x += y, gives us x = x + y, i.e., x = 100 + 50 = 150.
Now, again, x -= y equates to x = x – y, i.e., x = 150 – 50 = 100. In the same fashion, we can understand other statements.

Logical

These operators are used to perform logical operations such as AND, OR, and NOT. They are often clubbed with conditional statements to create much more complex conditional expressions. Given below is a table consisting of different logical operators along with their descriptions and syntax.

Operator	Description	Syntax
and (logical AND)	It returns a True value if both operands are True.	x and y
or (logical OR)	It returns a True value if either one operand or both operands are True.	x or y
not (logical NOT)	It returns a True value if the operand is False or it returns a False value if the operand is True.	not x

We can understand it using an example such as:

```
*Operators.py - C:\Users\Saurabh Gupta\AppData\Local\Programs\Python\Python39\Operators.py (3.9.2)*          —    □    ×
File  Edit  Format  Run  Options  Window  Help
x = True
y = False

print(x and y)

print(x or y)

print(not x)

print(not y)
```

Upon execution of the script, the output will be shown as:

```
= RESTART: C:\Users\Saurabh Gupta\AppData\Local\Programs\Python\Python39\Operato
rs.py
False
True
False
True
>>>
```

In the case of the *'and'* operator, because one of the values is False, it returns a False.

In the case of the *'or'* operator, because one of the values is True, it returns a True.

In the case of the *'not'* operator, it returns the opposite value of the given value.

Bitwise

These operators are used to perform bit-by-bit operations on binary numbers. Following are the bitwise operators supported by Python, listed in a tabular form along, with their syntax.

Operator	Syntax
& (Bitwise AND)	x & y
| (Bitwise OR)	x | y
^ (Bitwise XOR)	x ^ y
~ (Bitwise NOT)	~ x
<< (Bitwise left shift)	x << y
>> (Bitwise right shift)	x >> y

To understand bitwise operations, one must know about binary arithmetic and binary logic. Bitwise operators work on that logic. Let's see an example of how bitwise operators can be used in a Python program:

```
Operators.py - C:\Users\Saurabh Gupta\AppData\Local\Programs\Python\Python39\Operators.py (3.9.2)          —    □    ×
File  Edit  Format  Run  Options  Window  Help
x = 5
y = 2

print("Present value of x is: ",x)

print("Present value of y is: ",y)

print("The value after performing x&y is: ",x&y)

print("The value after performing x|y is: ",x|y)

print("The value after performing x^y is: ",x^y)

print("The value after performing ~x is: ",~x)

print("The value after performing x<<y is: ",x<<y)

print("The value after performing x>>y is: ",x>>y)
```

After we execute the script, the output will be:

```
>>>
= RESTART: C:\Users\Saurabh Gupta\AppData\Local\Programs\Python\Python39\Operato
rs.py
Present value of x is:  5
Present value of y is:  2
The value after performing x&y is:  0
The value after performing x|y is:  7
The value after performing x^y is:  7
The value after performing ~x is:  -6
The value after performing x<<y is:  20
The value after performing x>>y is:  1
>>>
```

Membership

These operators are used for validating the presence of an object inside a Python sequence such as string, list, tuple, array, etc. Python supports two membership operators that are listed below, along with their description and syntax.

Operator	Description	Syntax
In	It returns a True value when the object is present inside the sequence; otherwise, it returns False.	x in y
not in	It returns a True value when the object is absent inside the sequence; otherwise, it returns False.	x not in y

Let's try to understand this using an example.

Recall that we learned, in the previous chapter, that a list is a sequence-type data type that can hold items inside it. We can use a list to understand the concept of membership operator. We can check on whether or not an item exists in the list by using the membership operator, as in the following example:

```
Operators.py - C:\Users\Saurabh Gupta\AppData\Local\Programs\Python\Python39\Operators.py (3.9.2)    —    □    X
File  Edit  Format  Run  Options  Window  Help
x = [10,20,30,40,50]

print("Is 30 present in x?: ",(30 in x))

print("Is 60 present in x?: ",(60 in x))

print("Is 20 not present in x?: ",(30 not in x))

print("Is 55 not present in x?: ",(55 not in x))
```

Upon execution of the script, the output will be shown as:

```
IDLE Shell 3.9.2                                                    —    □    X
File  Edit  Shell  Debug  Options  Window  Help
Python 3.9.2 (tags/v3.9.2:1a79785, Feb 19 2021, 13:44:55) [MSC v.1928 64 bit (AM
D64)] on win32
Type "help", "copyright", "credits" or "license()" for more information.
>>>
= RESTART: C:\Users\Saurabh Gupta\AppData\Local\Programs\Python\Python39\Operato
rs.py
Is 30 present in x?:  True
Is 60 present in x?:  False
Is 20 not present in x?:  False
Is 55 not present in x?:  True
>>>
```

Identity

The operators that are used for validating whether two objects share the same memory location is called identity operator. Python supports two identity operators that are listed below along with their description and syntax.

Operator	Description	Syntax
is	It returns a True value when operands on both sides belong to the same memory location; otherwise, it returns False.	x is y
is not	It returns a True value when operands on both sides do not belong to the same memory location; otherwise, it returns False.	x is not y

Let's try to understand this using an example:

```
*Operators.py - C:\Users\Saurabh Gupta\AppData\Local\Programs\Python\Python39\Operators.py (3.9.2)*     —    □    ×
File  Edit  Format  Run  Options  Window  Help
x = 10
y = 10
z = x

print("Memory location of x is: ", id(x))

print("Memory location of y is: ", id(y))

print("Memory location of z is: ", id(z))

print("Does x and y represent same object?: ",(x is y))

print("Does x and z represent same object?: ",(x is z))

print("Does x and y represent different object?: ",(x is not y))

print("Does x and z represent different object?: ",(x is not z))
```

Upon execution of the script, the output will be shown as:

```
= RESTART: C:\Users\Saurabh Gupta\AppData\Local\Programs\Python\Python39\Operato
rs.py
Memory location of x is:  2103782566480
Memory location of y is:  2103782566480
Memory location of z is:  2103782566480
Does x and y represent same object?:  True
Does x and z represent same object?:  True
Does x and y represent different object?:  False
Does x and z represent different object?:  False
>>>
```

Note: We can use the id() function available in Python that returns the memory block at which an object is located. We can use it to verify that two variables (here, x and z) point to the same memory location.

Also, it should be noted that although variables x and y hold the same value, they do not point to the same memory location.

Precedence and Associativity Rule of Operators

When a Python statement consists of multiple operators, it must follow a specific rule to perform operations correctly. The precedence and associativity rule of operators allows us to determine the order of evaluation of operators inside a complex expression involving multiple operators. Below is a list of operators with their associativity property along with precedence order (in decreasing order), i.e., the operator that should get executed first is at the top and the one with the least preference is at the bottom of the table.

Operator	Description	Associativity
()	Parentheses	Left to right
**	Exponential (Power)	Right to left
+x, -x, ~x	Unary Addition, Unary Subtraction, Bitwise NOT	Left to right
*, /, //, %	Multiplication, Division, Floor Division, Modulus	Left to right
+, -	Arithmetic addition, Arithmetic subtraction	Left to right
<<, >>	Bitwise shift left, Bitwise shift right	Left to right
&	Bitwise AND	Left to right

^	Bitwise OR	Left to right
|	Bitwise XOR	Left to right
==, !=, >, >=, <, <=	Relational operators	Left to right
=, +=, -=, *=, /=, //=, **=, %=	Assignment and Augmented assignment operators	Right to Left
in, not, in, is, is not	Membership, Identity operators	Left to right
Not	Logical NOT	Left to right
And	Logical AND	Left to right
Or	Logical OR	Left to right

An Appeal from the Publisher

Hello wonderful reader!

We hope you are enjoying this book.

We wanted to let you know that you have made an impact on many lives by reading this book.

Just to give you a brief introduction: We are a small publishing company with a team of 8 writers and 2 editors.

Most of our employees come from financially weaker section and our company is the only means they support their families. This is our way of giving back to the society.

We don't have the giant advertising budgets that many other publishers and businesses do online.

So, one way that you can really support our mission and our business is by leaving us a review on this book.

For a small company like us, getting reviews (especially on Amazon) means we can submit our books for advertising.

This means we can actually sell a few copies from time to time and make a bigger impact on the society as a whole. So, every review means a lot to us.

We can't THANK YOU enough for this!

INTRODUCTION TO CONDITIONAL STATEMENTS AND LOOPS

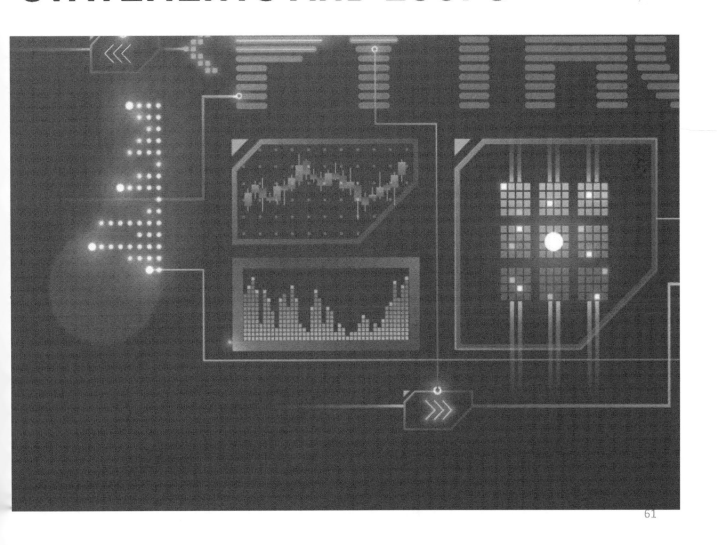

Having discussed so many things from scratch, let's get more into programming. You must have heard that programming is less about coding and more about logical thinking. That's 100% correct.

Programming is all about using logic to achieve a certain task and then coding this logic into some programming language and executing the program to achieve our desired result. But throughout all this, there will be certain situations in which we must make decisions and execute certain statements twice, thrice, or even multiple times.

So, for such situations, Python gives us the support for writing conditional statements for decision-making and loops for executing our statements multiple times. In this chapter, we will be reviewing these two concepts.

Statements in Python

Up to now, you must have been thinking that we are continuously talking about statements, but what does that actually mean? You need not worry. Those instructions that we write inside the program as a source code and that can get executed by the interpreter are called statements.

Conditional Statements/Decision-Making Statements

Those statements that help us decide the flow of execution of the program are called decision-making statements. The conditional statements are evaluated to a make decision based on the outcome that is in the form of either TRUE or FALSE.

It should be noted that Python interprets any non-zero/non-null values as TRUE, and FALSE otherwise in case of zero or null.

A general schematic representation of the decision-making can be represented as:

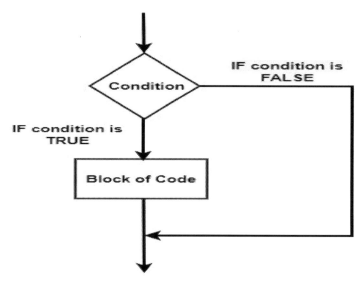

If Statement

The simplest form of decision-making statement is the if statement. If the condition is evaluated as TRUE, a certain set of statements will get executed inside the if block. Otherwise, if the condition is evaluated as FALSE, those sets of statements are skipped and will not get executed.

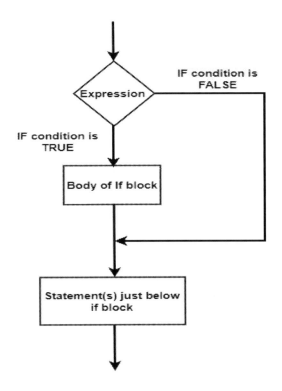

Syntax

if expression:

    ....

    Block of statements

    ....

A few important points to be remembered in the syntax:
We can write the conditional expression with or without round brackets
(). Then we use a delimiter semicolon (:) to mark the start of an
intended block in the if statement. We use an intended block that helps
to identify the set of statements to get executed if the condition
becomes True. Let's learn about this using an example program.
In this, we will ask the user to input a number. If the number is greater
than 0, the if block will get executed.

```
*if.py - C:/Users/Saurabh Gupta/AppData/Local/Programs/Python/Python39/if.py (3.9.2)*    —    □    ✕

File  Edit  Format  Run  Options  Window  Help
a = int(input("Enter a value: "))

if a>0:
    print("Value is greater than 0")
    print("If condition executed successfully")
```

In the above program, we have asked the user to enter a value using
the **input()** function. It should be kept in mind that the value entered
by the user is interpreted as a string by the interpreter. Hence, we use
the **int()** function to typecast the string data type to the integer data
type. Then we assign its value to the variable **'a'**. Now, we have used
the **if** keyword to make our conditional statement;

we created a condition that if the number entered by the user is greater than zero, only then will our body inside the if block get executed. Otherwise, it will be skipped and then the program will terminate automatically.

When we save and run the program on the IDLE, we will see that the interpreter asks us to enter a value. When you enter the value as 5, which is greater than 0, the if condition will be set to True. Hence, the print statement inside the intended block gets executed and then the program gets executed.

If we enter any value less than or equal to zero, the if condition will return False. Thus, the intended block will be skipped and nothing will get printed. The program terminates successfully.

```
= RESTART: C:/Users/Saurabh Gupta/AppData/Local/Programs/Python/Python39/if.py =
Enter a value: 5
Value is greater than 0
If condition executed successfully
>>>
>>>
= RESTART: C:/Users/Saurabh Gupta/AppData/Local/Programs/Python/Python39/if.py =
Enter a value: -1
>>>
>>> |
```

If-Else Statement

In the previous case, if the if block doesn't execute, the program terminates. What if we want that? Upon failure of the if block, some other set of statements will get executed. For this purpose, we use the else block. See the following flowchart:

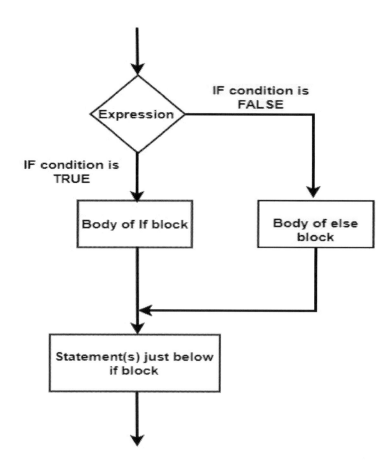

Syntax

if expression:

     ....

     Block of statements

     ....

else:

     ....

     Block of statements

     ....

Given below is a sample program to check if an entered number is even or odd:

```
if.py - C:\Users\Saurabh Gupta\AppData\Local\Programs\Python\Python39\if.py (3.9.2)    —    □    X
File  Edit  Format  Run  Options  Window  Help

a = int(input("Enter a number: "))

if a%2==0:
    print("Inside if block")
    print("Entered number is even")
else:
    print("Inside else block")
    print("Entered number is odd")
```

Upon executing the above program, once for an even number and a second time with an odd value, the output will be obtained as:

```
= RESTART: C:\Users\Saurabh Gupta\AppData\Local\Programs\Python\Python39\if.py =
Enter a number: 6
Inside if block
Entered number is even
>>>
>>>
= RESTART: C:\Users\Saurabh Gupta\AppData\Local\Programs\Python\Python39\if.py =
Enter a number: 3
Inside else block
Entered number is odd
>>>
```

If-Elif-Else Ladder

We can even use a ladder-type **if-elif-else** condition that lets us decide amongst multiple options. It is executed in a top-down manner starting with the **if** condition if it fails. Then we proceed forward with the **elif** condition(s). There can be a desired number of **elif** conditions and if all fails, finally the **else** block will get executed. It should be kept in mind while proceeding in a top-down manner that whenever a condition is satisfied and its block gets executed, all remaining blocks of the ladder will get skipped. Observe the following flowchart:

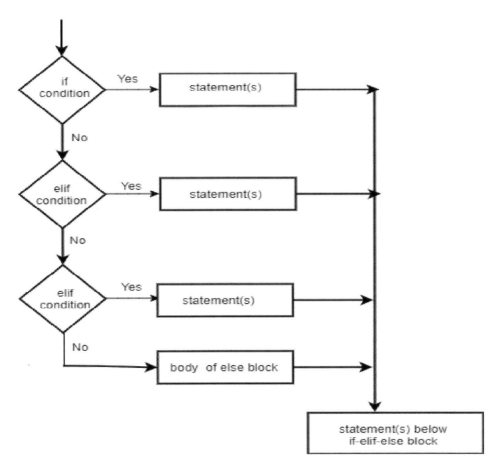

Syntax

if condition_1:

    Block of statement(s)

elif condition_2:

    Block of statement(s)

elif condition_3:

    Block of statement(s)

else:

    Block of statement(s)

Let's take a look at an example:

We will write a program to choose any one number between 1, 2, and 3. If one of these is selected, some specific block will get executed. If not, the else statement will get executed and it will say Invalid response.

```
if.py - C:\Users\Saurabh Gupta\AppData\Local\Programs\Python\Python39\if.py (3.9.2)          —  □  X
File  Edit  Format  Run  Options  Window  Help

a = int(input("Choose any of the one number 1, 2 and 3: "))

if (a == 1):
    print ("You entered 1")
elif (a == 2):
    print ("You entered 2")
elif (a == 3):
    print ("You entered 3")
else:
    print ("Invalid response")
```

Upon executing the program, the output will be generated as:

```
IDLE Shell 3.9.2                                                    —    □    ×

File  Edit  Shell  Debug  Options  Window  Help
Python 3.9.2 (tags/v3.9.2:1a79785, Feb 19 2021, 13:44:55) [MSC v.1928 64 bit (AM
D64)] on win32
Type "help", "copyright", "credits" or "license()" for more information.
>>>
= RESTART: C:\Users\Saurabh Gupta\AppData\Local\Programs\Python\Python39\if.py =
Choose any of the one number 1, 2 and 3: 1
You entered 1
>>>
>>>
= RESTART: C:\Users\Saurabh Gupta\AppData\Local\Programs\Python\Python39\if.py =
Choose any of the one number 1, 2 and 3: 2
You entered 2
>>>
>>>
= RESTART: C:\Users\Saurabh Gupta\AppData\Local\Programs\Python\Python39\if.py =
Choose any of the one number 1, 2 and 3: 3
You entered 3
>>>
= RESTART: C:\Users\Saurabh Gupta\AppData\Local\Programs\Python\Python39\if.py =
Choose any of the one number 1, 2 and 3: 4
Invalid response
>>> |
```

When the user chooses 1, first the if block will get executed and the rest of the other blocks will be skipped. If the user enters 2, the first if condition will fail and the control will go to the first elif block. It returns TRUE, so other blocks will get skipped and the program will terminate. In this way, the if-elif-else ladder works.

Nested If Statement

We can even make nested conditional statements by putting one if block inside another if block. This is useful when we want to make decisions based on some pre-existing condition. Take a look at the following flowchart to understand it more carefully:

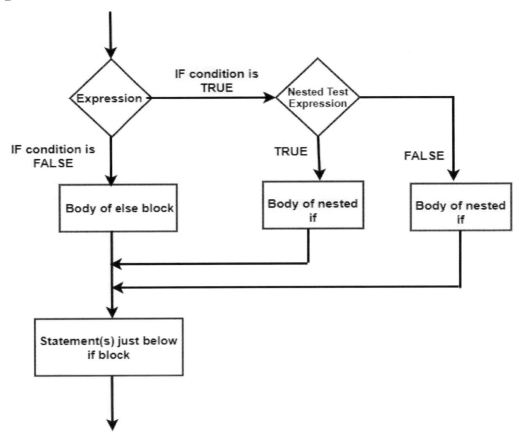

Syntax

if (condition_1):

    Execute statement(s) when condition1 is true

    if (condition_2):

        # Executes statement(s) when condition_2 is true

    # nested if block ends here

parent if block ends here

Let's have a look at one example:

```
a = int(input("Enter a number: "))

if (a == 1):
    print ("You entered 1")

    b = int(input("Enter a number: "))
    if (b == 2):
        print ("You entered 2")

print("Execution complete")
```

Output of the program upon running:

```
= RESTART: C:\Users\Saurabh Gupta\AppData\Local\Programs\Python\Python39\if.py =
Enter a number: 1
You entered 1
Enter a number: 2
You entered 2
Execution complete
>>>
>>>
= RESTART: C:\Users\Saurabh Gupta\AppData\Local\Programs\Python\Python39\if.py =
Enter a number: 1
You entered 1
Enter a number: 5
Execution complete
>>> |
```

Short-Hand If/If-Else Notation

We can even execute if or if-else conditionals in a single statement. The syntax can be written as:

- if condition : statement

  E.g., **if** a>0 : print("positive")

- [statement if condition is True] **if** condition **else** [statement if condition is False]

  E.g., print("positive") **if** a>0 else **print**("not positive")

Loops

Loops in a programming language are used to run a certain set of instructions iteratively. Python gives us primarily three different ways through which loops can be implemented inside the program.

- ➤ While loop
- ➤ For loop
- ➤ Nested loop (loop inside loop)

While Loop

While loops are used to iterate over a particular set of statements multiple times until the test condition becomes false. It is more suitable to use this loop when we do not know how many iterations we want to run the loop. That's why while loops fall under the category of indefinite iteration.

Syntax

while (conditional_expression):
        statement(s) to be iterated

Let's have a look at the flowchart of the while loop:

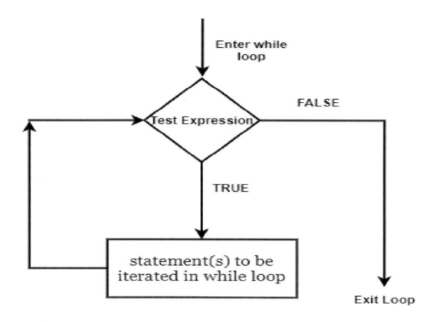

Let's have a look at one example, in which we will compute the first five powers of 2 using a while loop.

```
i = 1

while (i <= 5 ):
    print("Iteration : ",i)
    print("2 raised to the power %s = %s"%(i,2**i))
    i += 1

print("Program terminated successfully")
```

When we save and run this program, the output we obtain will look like this:

```
>>>
= RESTART: C:\Users\Saurabh Gupta\AppData\Local\Programs\Python\Python39\if.py =
Iteration :  1
2 raised to the power 1 = 2
Iteration :  2
2 raised to the power 2 = 4
Iteration :  3
2 raised to the power 3 = 8
Iteration :  4
2 raised to the power 4 = 16
Iteration :  5
2 raised to the power 5 = 32
Program terminated successfully
>>>
```

The program starts with i = 1, and the value of i increments by 1 every time the statements inside the while block are executed. As soon as the value of i becomes 6, the conditional expression inside the while loop sets off to False, the program flow exits the loop block, and the program is successfully terminated.

While Loop in a Single Statement

Just as we wrote one line of syntax for writing an if/if-else statement, we can write while loops in one line. Remember, in this case, if we want to have multiple statements inside our while block, they are separated by semi-colons(;).

while (conditional_expression): statement_1 to be iterated ; statement_2 to be iterated

For the previously given example of the while loop, a single-line statement can be written as:

```
i = 1

while (i <= 5 ): print("Iteration : ",i); print(2**i); i += 1

print("Program terminated successfully")
```

Upon execution of the program, the output will be shown as:

```
>>>
= RESTART: C:\Users\Saurabh Gupta\AppData\Local\Programs\Python\Python39\if.py =
Iteration :  1
2
Iteration :  2
4
Iteration :  3
8
Iteration :  4
16
Iteration :  5
32
Program terminated successfully
>>>
```

For Loop

The for loop is one of the most convenient ways to iterate over a sequence type or other iterable object in Python. That sequence can be List, String, Tuple, Dictionary, Set, etc.

Using the for loop, we can iterate into a sequence until we reach the end of the sequence. As soon as we enter the end of the sequence, we exit the loop. Iterating over a sequence type is also sometimes known as a traversal of the sequence. One of its advantages over the while loop is that it does not require an indexing variable to be set in the beginning.

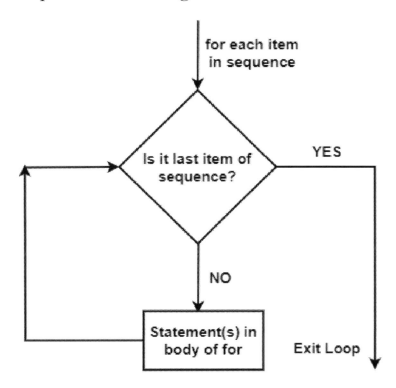

Syntax

for iter_var in sequence:
statement(s)

We require an additional iterating variable (here denoted by, iter_var) to iterate over the sequence.

Looping/Traversing Over a String Using For Loop

As we already discussed, the for loop can be used to traverse over sequences. In this part, we are going to see how the for loop traverses over a sequence of characters, i.e., a string.

```
str1 = "Hello_World"

for i in str1:
    print("Traversal reached upto letter: ",i)
```

We take a string and assign it to a variable named str1. Then, using a for loop, we traverse through all the characters/letters in the string one by one with the help of iterating variable i. As soon as we reach the end of the string, the loop terminates automatically. Upon executing the program, the output will be obtained as:

```
>>>
= RESTART: C:\Users\Saurabh Gupta\AppData\Local\Programs\Python\Python39\if.py =
Traversal reached upto letter:  H
Traversal reached upto letter:  e
Traversal reached upto letter:  l
Traversal reached upto letter:  l
Traversal reached upto letter:  o
Traversal reached upto letter:  _
Traversal reached upto letter:  W
Traversal reached upto letter:  o
Traversal reached upto letter:  r
Traversal reached upto letter:  l
Traversal reached upto letter:  d
>>>
```

For Loop With Else Block

A for loop can have an additional **else** block as well. The else block comes into use when the elements inside the sequence get exhausted.

Syntax

for iter_var in sequence:
statement(s)
else:
statement(s)

A sample example of a for...else block can be given as:

```
str1 = "Hello"

for i in str1:
    print("Traversal reached upto letter: ",i)

else:
    print("String traversal finished")
```

Output

From the output, we can observe, even after the elements in the for loop get exhausted, that **else** block statements get executed last.

```
= RESTART: C:\Users\Saurabh Gupta\AppData\Local\Programs\Python\Python39\if.py =
Traversal reached upto letter:  H
Traversal reached upto letter:  e
Traversal reached upto letter:  l
Traversal reached upto letter:  l
Traversal reached upto letter:  o
String traversal finished
>>>
```

Nested Loops

We can even implement the nesting of loops, in which we can implement one or more loops inside another loop. One more interesting feature is that we can place any loop inside another loop, i.e., we can place a while loop inside a for loop and vice-versa.

Syntax for nested while loop

while (conditional_expression):
    while (conditional_expression):
        statement(s) to be iterated
    statement(s) to be iterated

Syntax for nested for loop

for iter_var in sequence:
    for iter_var in sequence:
        statement(s) to be iterated
    statement(s) to be iterated

An example of nesting of loops:

We will write a program to understand the concept of nesting of loops. We will loop through two different lists, named 'category' and 'Veggies', and try to access each element in Veggies first by category 1 and then by category 2.

```
Veggies = ['Potato', 'Cabbage', 'Lady Finger']

category = [1,2]

for x in category:
    for y in Veggies:
        print(x,y)
```

When we run the program, we will observe that the outer loop begins with category 1 and then the inner loop traverses all the elements inside the Veggies list. After the elements in the Veggies list get exhausted, the inner loop stops, and the control goes back to the outer loop.

It starts with category 2 and then the inner loop lists all the elements inside the Veggies list. Once again, the control will go back to the outer loop, but now elements inside the category list will also exhaust, so the outer loop will also stop and the program terminates successfully. The output can be shown as:

```
= RESTART: C:\Users\Saurabh Gupta\AppData\Local\Programs\Python\Python39\if.py =
1 Potato
1 Cabbage
1 Lady Finger
2 Potato
2 Cabbage
2 Lady Finger
>>> |
```

Loop Control Statements

Loop control statements in Python are a useful tool for manipulating the flow of execution of statements inside a loop. Python supports three types of loop control statements, which are listed below:

i. Break statement

A break keyword is used to terminate the currently running loop. It transfers the control to the next block. If we use a break statement inside a nested loop, the control exits from the innermost loop. The control goes back to the next statement out of that block. It can be used inside both for and while loops.

For example, in this program, we will traverse through a list and print its elements. If the element inside the list is equal to 4, the if condition becomes True and, thus, the break statement will get executed. Hence, the control of the for loop breaks, and the loop gets terminated after we reach 4.

```python
Sno = [1,2,3,4,5,6]

for i in Sno:
    print(i)

    if i == 4:
        break

print('Loop terminated')
```

Output

```
>>>
= RESTART: C:\Users\Saurabh Gupta\AppData\Local\Programs\Python\Python39\if.py =
1
2
3
4
Loop terminated
>>> |
```

ii. Continue statement

The continue statement transfers control of the block to the beginning of the loop. It is used with both the while loop and for loop. When the continue statement inside the block is executed, it leaves the remaining statements inside the block and transfers the control to the starting of the loop.

Example of continue statement inside a for loop:

```
Sno = [1,2,3,4,5,6]

for i in Sno:
    print(i)

    if i == 4:
        print('Executed inside if block')
        continue
        print('Control sent back to the top')

print('Loop terminated')
```

When we run this code, the output we get is shown below. When the loop goes to 4 and the if condition becomes true, it executes the first print statement, and then it encounters the continue statement. As soon as it executes the continue statement, the control goes back to the start of the loop and the second print statement inside the i9f block gets skipped.

```
= RESTART: C:\Users\Saurabh Gupta\AppData\Local\Programs\Python\Python39\if.py =
1
2
3
4
Executed inside if block
5
6
Loop terminated
>>>
```

iii. Pass statement

The pass statement is used at places where we must write some statements syntactically for execution but we do not write anything. When the pass statement gets executed, no change will take place; it is a form of null operation.

Example of pass statement inside a for loop:

```
Sno = [1,2,3,4,5,6]

for i in Sno:
    pass
print('Loop terminated')
```

Output

```
= RESTART: C:\Users\Saurabh Gupta\AppData\Local\Programs\Python\Python39\if.py =
Loop terminated
>>>
```

We can see in the output that the **pass** statement simply passes the flow of loop to the next block without throwing any error. If there hadn't been a pass statement in the **for** loop, the interpreter would throw an error saying that an intended block is expected.

LISTS, TUPLES, AND DICTIONARIES

Lists

You have already been introduced to lists in chapter 3, where we discussed lists as one of the sequence data types. Apart from being a data type, a list is considered a data structure in Python because of its ability to hold data items inside it.   The list is non-homogenous and can store data of different types. One of the key properties of the list is that it is mutable, which means it can be altered even after its declaration. This makes it one of the most frequently used data structures in Python. It is analogous to widely used dynamic arrays such as Vectors in C++ and ArrayList in Java.

Lists are linear and ordered in nature and the elements stored inside a list are stored following a particular order. These elements can be accessed using indices. Usually, the indexing of a list starts from the 0th index.

Creating a List

To create a list, we just need to enclose elements inside the square ([]) brackets and separate them using commas. As already discussed, elements can be of any data type— strings, integers, floats, Boolean, etc. It should be noted that when we have a list containing another list inside it, we call it a **nested list**.

Creating a list holding some alphabetical characters can be done as follows:

List_1 = [' a', 'b', 'c', 'y', 'z']

It can be pictorially represented as:

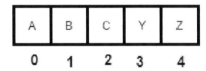

Here, the numbers shown at the bottom of the list are its indices. These indices will always be of type integers and can't be any other data type, such as float, string, etc.

Also, it should be noted that elements are stored starting from the 0th index, i.e., the first element is at the 0th index, the second element will be at the 1st index, and so on.

Accessing Elements Inside a List

Elements inside a list can be accessed via the index operator [] by making use of its indices. Let's see a Python program to create and access its elements inside a list.

```
list_1 = ['A', 'B', 'C', 'Y', 'Z']

print('Element at 0th index is: ', list_1[0])

print('Element at 1st index is: ', list_1[1])

print('Element at 2nd index is: ', list_1[2])

print('Element at 4th index is: ', list_1[4])
```

In the program, we have first created a list of characters and assigned to a variable named list_1. Then we have made use of the indices to access elements from the list. The output of the program after the running and executing of the script can be shown as:

```
= RESTART: C:\Users\Saurabh Gupta\AppData\Local\Programs\Python\Python39\if.py =
Element at 0th index is:  A
Element at 1st index is:  B
Element at 2nd index is:  C
Element at 4th index is:  Z
>>> |
```

Negative Indexing in Python

So far, we have used only positive indices to access elements inside the list. Now we will see one more interesting notation, using which elements inside the sequences can be numbered in Python. These are in reverse order using the negative indices. The list we made earlier can be represented using negative indices as:

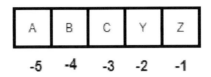

Let's revisit the same program we wrote earlier and make some modifications to it to access those elements using negative indices.

```python
list_1 = ['A', 'B', 'C', 'Y', 'Z']

print('First element from the last is : ', list_1[-1])

print('Second element from the last is: ', list_1[-2])

print('Third element from the last is: ', list_1[-3])

print('Fourth element from the last is: ', list_1[-4])
```

The output of the above-given source code upon execution will be:

```
= RESTART: C:\Users\Saurabh Gupta\AppData\Local\Programs\Python\Python39\if.py =
First element from the last is :  Z
Second element from the last is:  Y
Third element from the last is:  C
Fourth element from the last is:  B
>>>
```

Thus, we can see how positive and negative indices can both be used effectively to access the elements stored inside a list.

Note: If we try to access indices that are not in the list, the interpreter will throw an IndexError. Also, if we try to put any other value apart from integers in the index field, the interpreter will throw TypeError.

Slicing in List

Slicing in list is used to return a range of elements from the list. The semicolon (:) symbol is used as the slicing operator. The general syntax for slicing is given as [start:stop]. Furthermore, one more advanced syntax is [start:stop:step].

Let's try to understand the basic syntax first. Then we will proceed forward to the advanced syntax.

Start inside the basic syntax can be interpreted as the index from where we want to start slicing, while stop is the index up to where we want to slice. Here, one important thing to be kept in mind is that the start index is inclusive of the range and the stop value is exclusive to the range, i.e., we return the sequence from the start index to the stop-1 index. For a better understanding, let's look at an example:

```
list_1 = ['A', 'B', 'C', 'Y', 'Z','M','N','O']

print('Elements starting from oth index to 3rd index can be returned using: ', list_1[0:4])

print('Elements starting from 1st index to 4th index can be returned using: ', list_1[1:5])

print('Elements starting from 3rd index to the 6th index can be returned using: ', list_1[3:7])

print('Elements starting from the 0th index to 5th index can be returned using: ', list_1[:6])

print('Elements starting from 3rd index to the last index can be returned using: ', list_1[3:])

print('Complete list can be returned using: ', list_1[:])
```

When we save and run this program, the output will be generated as:

```
>>>
= RESTART: C:\Users\Saurabh Gupta\AppData\Local\Programs\Python\Python39\if.py =
Elements starting from oth index to 3rd index can be returned using:  ['A', 'B', 'C', 'Y']
Elements starting from 1st index to 4th index can be returned using:  ['B', 'C', 'Y', 'Z']
Elements starting from 3rd index to the 6th index can be returned using:  ['Y', 'Z', 'M', 'N']
Elements starting from the 0th index to 5th index can be returned using:  ['A', 'B', 'C', 'Y', 'Z', 'M']
Elements starting from 3rd index to the last index can be returned using:  ['Y', 'Z', 'M', 'N', 'O']
Complete list can be returned using:  ['A', 'B', 'C', 'Y', 'Z', 'M', 'N', 'O']
>>>
```

As discussed earlier, we can see how the slicing operator works on the list. Also, if you observe the last three examples, you can see that if we don't pass an index value in the **start** position, it implicitly takes its value from the 0th index. Similarly, if we don't pass any index value at the **stop** place, it will implicitly take it to be the last item in the list.

Now that we know the basic syntax of the slice operator on the list, let's move ahead with the advanced syntax, i.e., [**start: stop: step**]. Here, an additional **step** index is added that is used for skipping elements in the sequence. Look at the code snippet given below:

```
list_1 = ['A', 'B', 'C', 'Y', 'Z','M','N','O']

print('Elements starting from oth index to 3rd index with step 2: ', list_1[0:4:2])

print('Elements starting from 1st index to 7th index with step 3: ', list_1[1:7:3])

print('Elements starting from 3rd index to the 6th index with step 2: ', list_1[3:7:2])

print('Elements starting from the 0th index to last index with step 3: ', list_1[::3])

```

The output we will get after running the program will be shown as:

```
Elements starting from oth index to 3rd index with step 2:  ['A', 'C']
Elements starting from 1st index to 7th index with step 3:  ['B', 'Z']
Elements starting from 3rd index to the 6th index with step 2:  ['Y', 'M']
Elements starting from the 0th index to last index with step 3:  ['A', 'Y', 'N']
>>> 
```

When the **step** value is given as 2, every second element in the sequence gets skipped. Thus, we can see that elements get skipped using the **step** value.

Note: List slicing can also be done by making use of negative indices.

Manipulating Elements Inside a List

1. Updating the values inside the list

Lists are mutable, so we can make changes to a list even after we declare them beforehand. We can use the assignment operator to make changes inside the pre-declared list. We can update a specific element inside a list or a sequence of elements inside the list. See the following example:

```
list_1 = ['A', 'B', 'C', 'Y', 'Z','M','N','O']

print('Original list_1 is: ',list_1)

# Updating element at oth index, replacing 'A' by 1
list_1[0] = 1

# Updating element at 2nd index, replacing 'C' by 10
list_1[2] = 10

# Updating element at 5th index, replacing 'M' by 100
list_1[5] = 100


print('Updated list_1 is: ',list_1)


list_2 = [1,10,100,90,80,70,50,25,75,125]

print('Original list_2 is: ',list_2)

# Updating sequence from 0th to 4th index in list_2
list_2[0:5] = 'A', 'B','C','D','E'

print('Updated list is: ',list_2)
```

First, we are updating specific elements inside list_1 and then we are updating a sequence of elements in list_2. Appropriate comments are placed over each of the lines to help you better understand each line of code.

Note: Writing comments at appropriate places helps readers to easily understand your code; it is a good coding practice to write comments. Comments are not displayed as an output on the console. We can use the (#) symbol to write one-line comments.

Output

```
= RESTART: C:\Users\Saurabh Gupta\AppData\Local\Programs\Python\Python39\if.py =
Original list_1 is:  ['A', 'B', 'C', 'Y', 'Z', 'M', 'N', 'O']
Updated list_1 is:  [1, 'B', 10, 'Y', 'Z', 100, 'N', 'O']
Original list_2 is:  [1, 10, 100, 90, 80, 70, 50, 25, 75, 125]
Updated list is:  ['A', 'B', 'C', 'D', 'E', 70, 50, 25, 75, 125]
>>>
```

2. Adding elements to a list

As lists are dynamic, we can even add elements inside an already declared list. This can be done using any of the following given methods:

o **Using append() method**

We can use the built-in append() method to insert one element at a time inside a list. To insert multiple elements at a time, we must use a loop. This method appends the elements at the end of the list.

It could be done as:

```python
list_1 = ['A', 'B', 'C', 'Y']

print('Original list_1 is: ',list_1)

# Inserting element 1 in list_1
list_1.append(1)

# Inserting element 10 in list_1
list_1.append(10)

# Inserting element 100 in list_1
list_1.append(100)


print('Updated list_1 is: ',list_1)
```

Output

```
>>>
= RESTART: C:\Users\Saurabh Gupta\AppData\Local\Programs\Python\Python39\if.py =
Original list_1 is:  ['A', 'B', 'C', 'Y']
Updated list_1 is:  ['A', 'B', 'C', 'Y', 1, 10, 100]
>>>
```

o **Using insert() method**

We can use the insert() method to insert elements inside the list at the desired location. The insert() method takes in two arguments (position, value), where position denotes the index location and value is the element we want to insert. It is different from append() because the append() method always inserts elements at the end of the list. This is not the case here.

```
list_1 = ['A', 'B', 'C', 'Y']

print('Original list_1 is: ',list_1)

# Inserting element 10 at index 1 in list_1
list_1.insert(1, 10)

print('Updated list_1 is: ',list_1)

# Inserting element 50 at index 3 in list_1
list_1.insert(3, 50)

print('Updated list_1 is: ',list_1)
```

Output

```
= RESTART: C:\Users\Saurabh Gupta\AppData\Local\Programs\Python\Python39\if.py =
Original list_1 is:  ['A', 'B', 'C', 'Y']
Updated list_1 is:  ['A', 10, 'B', 'C', 'Y']
Updated list_1 is:  ['A', 10, 'B', 50, 'C', 'Y']
>>>
```

o **Using extend() method**

The extend() method can be used to add multiple elements at the same time inside a list. All the elements will be appended at the end of the list. Let's see a sample program to understand it.

```
list_1 = ['A', 'B', 'C', 'Y']

print('Original list_1 is: ',list_1)

# Inserting multiple elements at the end in list_1
list_1.extend([10,20,30,40])

print('Updated list_1 is: ',list_1)
```

Output

```
= RESTART: C:\Users\Saurabh Gupta\AppData\Local\Programs\Python\Python39\if.py =
Original list_1 is:  ['A', 'B', 'C', 'Y']
Updated list_1 is:  ['A', 'B', 'C', 'Y', 10, 20, 30, 40]
>>>
```

3. Removing/deleting elements from a list

Python provides us with two of the methods, using which we can remove elements from the list. These are discussed below:

- **Using pop() method**

  The pop() method can be used to remove one element at a time from the list. It implicitly removes the last element from a list. If we want to remove any element from a specific index, we must specify its index as an argument inside the pop() method. Let's try to understand it better using the program given below:

```python
list_1 = ['A', 'B', 'C', 'Y',10,20,30,'XYZ']

print('Original list_1 is: ',list_1)

# Popping an element from the end in list_1
list_1.pop()

print('Updated list_1 after popping an element: ',list_1)

# Popping element from the end in list_1
list_1.pop()

print('Updated list_1 after popping an element: ',list_1)

# Popping element at index 4 from the list
list_1.pop(4)

print('Updated list_1 after popping an element at 4th index: ',list_1)

# Popping element at index 1 from the list
list_1.pop(1)

print('Updated list_1 after popping an element at 1st index: ',list_1)

```

Output

```
= RESTART: C:\Users\Saurabh Gupta\AppData\Local\Programs\Python\Python39\if.py =
Original list_1 is:  ['A', 'B', 'C', 'Y', 10, 20, 30, 'XYZ']
Updated list_1 after popping an element:  ['A', 'B', 'C', 'Y', 10, 20, 30]
Updated list_1 after popping an element:  ['A', 'B', 'C', 'Y', 10, 20]
Updated list_1 after popping an element at 4th index:  ['A', 'B', 'C', 'Y', 20]
Updated list_1 after popping an element at 1st index:  ['A', 'C', 'Y', 20]
>>> |
```

- ## Using remove() method

  The remove() method works exactly opposite to the append()
  method. It can be used to remove one element at a time from the
  list. This method accepts a value that we want to remove from the
  list. If the value is not found in the list, it throws a ValueError. One
  point is to be noted: that if there are multiple same values inside the
  list, the only first same value is removed from the list. Its functioning
  can be seen in the following code snippet:

```
list_1 = ['A', 'B', 'C', 'Y',10,20,30,'XYZ']

print('Original list_1 is: ',list_1)

# Removing an element 1 from the list_1
list_1.remove(10)

print('Updated list_1 after removing 10: ',list_1)

# Removing an element 'B' from the list_1
list_1.remove('B')

print('Updated list_1 after removing B: ',list_1)
```

Output

```
= RESTART: C:\Users\Saurabh Gupta\AppData\Local\Programs\Python\Python39\if.py =
Original list_1 is:  ['A', 'B', 'C', 'Y', 10, 20, 30, 'XYZ']
Updated list_1 after removing 10:  ['A', 'B', 'C', 'Y', 20, 30, 'XYZ']
Updated list_1 after removing B:  ['A', 'C', 'Y', 20, 30, 'XYZ']
>>>
```

- **Using del keyword**

  We can use the del keyword to delete elements inside a list in Python. Its usage is depicted in the following source code:

```python
list_1 = ['A', 'B', 'C', 'Y',10,20,30,'XYZ']

print('Original list_1 is: ',list_1)

# Removing an element at index 0 from the list_1
del list_1[0]

print('Updated list_1 after removal: ',list_1)

# Removing an element at index 3 from the list_1
del list_1[3]

print('Updated list_1 after removal: ',list_1)
```

Output

```
= RESTART: C:\Users\Saurabh Gupta\AppData\Local\Programs\Python\Python39\if.py =
Original list_1 is:  ['A', 'B', 'C', 'Y', 10, 20, 30, 'XYZ']
Updated list_1 after removal:  ['B', 'C', 'Y', 10, 20, 30, 'XYZ']
Updated list_1 after removal:  ['B', 'C', 'Y', 20, 30, 'XYZ']
>>> |
```

Built-In Functions and Methods of List

A few built-in functions are used along with a list to get certain outputs that are discussed in the table below:

Function Name	Description
len(list)	It returns the total number of elements present inside a list.
list(sequence)	It is a list constructor that takes tuple sequences as inputs and converts them into a list.
max(list)	It returns the maximum element inside a list.
min(list)	It returns the minimum element inside a list.
cmp(list1,list2)	These are used to compare two lists.

List also supports multiple methods for performing different actions using the lists that are discussed below:

Method Name	Syntax	Description
append()	list.append(value)	It appends the given value to the end of the list.
extend()	list.extend(sequence)	It appends the given tuple/list sequence to the end of the list.
insert()	list.insert(index,value)	It inserts the given value at the specified index in the list.

Built-In Functions and Methods of List

Method Name	Syntax	Description
pop()	list.pop(value)	It removes the last item from the list, or if the value is given, it removes that value from the list.
remove()	list.remove(value)	It removes the given value from the first occurring place in the list.
count()	list.count(value)	It returns the count of the value passed as an argument inside the list.
index()	list.index(value)	It returns the index of the first matched value in the list.
reverse()	list.reverse()	It reverses the items present inside the list.
clear()	list.clear()	It removes all the elements from the list.
sort()	list.sort()	It sorts the elements present in a list in ascending order.
copy()	list.copy()	It returns a shallow copy of the list.

Basic Operations Over Lists

Python Expression	Result	Description
[10,20,30] + [40,50,60]	[10,20,30,40,50,60]	The +operator concatenates two lists side by side.
['A'] * 4	['A', 'A', 'A', 'A']	The multiply operator duplicates the same list multiple times inside the list.
1o in [10,20,30]	True	in is a membership operator that is used to check if a specified element is present in list.
40 not in [10,20,30]	True	not in is a membership operator that is used to check if a specified element is present in list.
for i in [10,20,30]: print(i)	10 20 30	The for loop can be used for operation over lists.

Tuples

A tuple in Python is an ordered collection of objects. These also belong to the sequence data types like lists. Unlike lists, tuples are immutable, i.e., they cannot be changed after they are declared.

Creating a Tuple

Tuples can easily be created by putting elements inside parentheses/round brackets (()). The elements are separated from each other using the comma symbol. Indices in Tuples also start with 0, where the first element is placed at the 0th index.

We can create nested tuples by putting a tuple inside another tuple. Creating a tuple that holds some alphabetical characters can be done as follows:
tuple_1 = (' a', 'b', 'c', 'y', 'z')

Note: If we have only a single element inside a tuple, we must place a comma value after the element to indicate that it is a tuple.
tuple_2 = ('Ram',) is the correct way instead of tuple_2 = ('Ram'). The former one with a comma after the element is interpreted as a tuple, whereas the latter one is interpreted as a string by the interpreter. To understand this, take a look at the following code snippet:

```
tuple_1 = ('A', 'B', 'C', 'Y')

print(type(tuple_1))

print('Original tuple_1 is: ',tuple_1)

tuple_2 = ('Ram',)
print(type(tuple_2))

tuple_3 = ('Ram')
print(type(tuple_3))
```

Output

```
= RESTART: C:\Users\Saurabh Gupta\AppData\Local\Programs\Python\Python39\if.py =
<class 'tuple'>
Original tuple_1 is:  ('A', 'B', 'C', 'Y')
<class 'tuple'>
<class 'str'>
>>>
```

We can see how variables tuple_2 and tuple_3 are interpreted differently by the interpreter.

Accessing elements inside a tuple

Just like we did in the case of list, we can use both the positive indices and negative indices to access elements stored inside a tuple. Given below is a code snippet showing how it can be done.

```
tuple_1 = ('A', 'B', 'C', 'Y')

print('Original tuple_1 is: ',tuple_1)

print('Printing the first element at 0th index: ',tuple_1[0])

print('Printing the second element at 1st index: ',tuple_1[1])

print('Printing the fourth element at 3rd index: ',tuple_1[3])

print('Printing the first element from last: ',tuple_1[-1])

print('Printing the third element from last: ',tuple_1[-3])
```

The output of the above-given source code will be given as

```
= RESTART: C:\Users\Saurabh Gupta\AppData\Local\Programs\Python\Python39\if.py =
Original tuple_1 is:  ('A', 'B', 'C', 'Y')
Printing the first element at 0th index:  A
Printing the second element at 1st index:  B
Printing the fourth element at 3rd index:  Y
Printing the first element from last:  Y
Printing the third element from last:  B
>>> |
```

Tuple Slicing

Tuple slicing can be used to obtain a sequence of elements from the tuple. It can be done in the same manner that we used for lists. Take a look at the following example:

```
tuple_1 = ('A', 'B', 'C', 'Y',1,10,100,50,'Ram','Bob')

print('Original tuple_1 is: ',tuple_1)

print('Printing elements starting from 0th index to 3rd index: ',tuple_1[0:4])

print('Printing elements starting from 2nd index to 5th index: ',tuple_1[2:6])

print('Printing elements starting from 1st index to 6th index with step 2: ',tuple_1[1:7:2])

print('Printing elements starting from 0th index to the last index with step 3: ',tuple_1[::3])
```

Output

```
= RESTART: C:\Users\Saurabh Gupta\AppData\Local\Programs\Python\Python39\if.py =
Original tuple_1 is:  ('A', 'B', 'C', 'Y', 1, 10, 100, 50, 'Ram', 'Bob')
Printing elements starting from 0th index to 3rd index:  ('A', 'B', 'C', 'Y')
Printing elements starting from 2nd index to 5th index:  ('C', 'Y', 1, 10)
Printing elements starting from 1st index to 6th index with step 2:  ('B', 'Y', 10)
Printing elements starting from 0th index to the last index with step 3:  ('A', 'Y', 100, 'Bob')
>>>
```

Manipulating Elements Inside a Tuple

1. Updating the values inside a tuple

As tuples are immutable, we cannot use the assignment operator to update values inside a tuple.

Suppose we have a tuple:

tuple_1 = ('A', 'B', 'C', 10, 100, 50) and we want to update the element at index 1, i.e., the character 'B' with a character 'M', it cannot be done using the assignment operator as:

tuple_1 [1] = 'M' (it is wrong; the interpreter will generate a TypeError in this case)
However, if the tuples consist of any mutable object inside it, then that object can be manipulated.

Also, we can use the '+' and '*' operator to perform concatenation and repetition of the elements present inside the tuple. Let's take a look at the following example:

```
tuple_1 = ('A', 'B', 'C')
tuple_2 = (10,100,50)

print('Original tuple_1 is: ',tuple_1)

print('Original tuple_2 is: ',tuple_2)

tuple_3 = tuple_1 + tuple_2

print('resultant tuple after concatenation is', tuple_3)

tuple_4 = tuple_2 * 3

print('resultant tuple_2 after repetition is', tuple_4)
```

Output

```
= RESTART: C:\Users\Saurabh Gupta\AppData\Local\Programs\Python\Python39\if.py =
Original tuple_1 is:  ('A', 'B', 'C')
Original tuple_2 is:  (10, 100, 50)
resultant tuple after concatenation is ('A', 'B', 'C', 10, 100, 50)
resultant tuple_2 after repetition is (10, 100, 50, 10, 100, 50, 10, 100, 50)
>>>
```

2. Removing/deleting elements from a tuple

As discussed earlier, elements inside a tuple can't be updated, so we cannot remove a particular element from a tuple. However, removing the entire tuple is possible. It could be done using the del keyword. Let's look at the following example:

```python
tuple_1 = ('A', 'B', 'C')

print('Original tuple_1 is: ',tuple_1)

del tuple_1

print(tuple_1)
```

Output

```
= RESTART: C:\Users\Saurabh Gupta\AppData\Local\Programs\Python\Python39\if.py =
Original tuple_1 is:  ('A', 'B', 'C')
Traceback (most recent call last):
  File "C:\Users\Saurabh Gupta\AppData\Local\Programs\Python\Python39\if.py", li
ne 7, in <module>
    print(tuple_1)
NameError: name 'tuple_1' is not defined
>>>
```

We can notice here, after we use the del keyword to remove the entire tuple, and then try to print it, the interpreter throws us a NameError saying it is not defined.

Built-In Tuple Functions and Methods

A few built-in functions are used with tuples to get certain outputs that are discussed in the table below:

Function Name	Description
len(tuple)	It returns the total number of elements present inside a tuple.
tuple(sequence)	It is a tuple constructor that takes list as inputs and converts them into a tuple.
max(tuple)	It returns the maximum element inside a tuple.
min(tuple)	It returns the minimum element inside a tuple.
cmp(tuple 1, tuple 2)	These are used to compare two tuples.

Also, we can use the in and not in operator to take the membership test, as we read in the case of lists.

Advantages of Tuple Over List

The immutable property of tuples makes it advantageous over lists in a variety of ways that are listed below:

- In terms of speed, it is faster to iterate through a tuple as compared to a list. This creates a slight boost in performance.
- Because tuples are immutable, they can be used as keys inside dictionaries.
- Tuples are generally used for storing heterogeneous data types, whereas lists are used for storing homogenous data types.
- If we want our data to be write-protected (it can't be manipulated), we keep it inside tuples.

Dictionaries

A dictionary is a kind of data structure that holds data in the form of key:value pairs where each key can hold a single value. The key values must be immutable; the supported data types for the keys are integers, strings, and tuples. Each key inside the dictionary should be unique.

Note: As of Python version 3.7 and above, dictionary elements inside the dictionary are kept in an ordered manner, while in earlier versions below 3.6, elements inside dictionaries were unordered.

Creating a Dictionary

A dictionary can be created by placing items as key:value pairs inside curly braces { }; the elements are separated by commas. A dictionary can have duplicate values of any data type, but keys must be unique and immutable. Given below is a source code explaining the creation of dictionaries in Python.

```
dict_1 = {'key1': 'value1', 'key2': 'value2', 'key3': 'value3', 'key4': 'value4'}

print('Elements in dict_1 are: ',dict_1)

dict_2 = {'Fruit': ['Apple','Mango','Guava'], 1: 'First', 2: 'Second', 'Name': 'Michael'}

print('Elements in dict_2 are: ',dict_2)
```

Output

```
>>>
= RESTART: C:\Users\Saurabh Gupta\AppData\Local\Programs\Python\Python39\if.py =
Elements in dict_1 are:  {'key1': 'value1', 'key2': 'value2', 'key3': 'value3', 'key4': 'value4'}
Elements in dict_2 are:  {'Fruit': ['Apple', 'Mango', 'Guava'], 1: 'First', 2: 'Second', 'Name': 'Michael'}
>>>
```

Output

```python
dictionary = dict({1: 'Ram', 2: 'Shyam', 3:'Mohan'})

print('Dictionary created using dict: ',dictionary)

dictionary_2 = dict([(1, 'Sam'),(2, 'Karan'),(3, 'Jai')])
print("Dictionary with each item as a pair: ",dictionary_2)
```

We can see the second example in the source code where the dict()
function is used to convert a list of tuples into a dictionary. The
output of the source code upon running will be obtained as:

```
= RESTART: C:\Users\Saurabh Gupta\AppData\Local\Programs\Python\Python39\if.py =
Dictionary created using dict:  {1: 'Ram', 2: 'Shyam', 3: 'Mohan'}
Dictionary with each item as a pair:  {1: 'Sam', 2: 'Karan', 3: 'Jai'}
>>>
```

Accessing Elements Inside a Dictionary

Unlike list and tuple, we don't use indices to access elements stored inside dictionaries. To access elements inside the dictionaries, we use the unique Keys. Take a look at the following example:

```python
dict_1 = {1: 'Ram', 2: 'Shyam', 'Name':'Mohan','Surname':'Sharma'}

print('Value having key 1 inside the dictionary: ',dict_1[1])

print('Value having key Name inside the dictionary: ',dict_1['Name'])

print('Value having key Surname inside the dictionary: ',dict_1['Surname'])
```

Output

```
= RESTART: C:\Users\Saurabh Gupta\AppData\Local\Programs\Python\Python39\if.py =
Value having key 1 inside the dictionary:  Ram
Value having key Name inside the dictionary:  Mohan
Value having key Surname inside the dictionary:  Sharma
>>>
```

If the key will not be present in the dictionary, the interpreter will throw us a KeyError.

Updating Elements in a Dictionary

We can modify an existing dictionary by updating the current value of an element present in the dictionary. It can be done as follows:

```python
dict_1 = {1: 'Ram', 2: 'Shyam', 'Name':'Mohan','Surname':'Sharma'}

print('Original dict_1 dictionary: ',dict_1)

# Updating the value having key as Name
dict_1['Name'] = 'Michael'

# Updating the value having key as Surname
dict_1['Surname'] = 'Jordan'

print('Updated dict_1 dictionary: ',dict_1)
```

Output of the code:

```
= RESTART: C:\Users\Saurabh Gupta\AppData\Local\Programs\Python\Python39\if.py =
Original dict_1 dictionary:  {1: 'Ram', 2: 'Shyam', 'Name': 'Mohan', 'Surname': 'Sharma'}
Updated dict_1 dictionary:  {1: 'Ram', 2: 'Shyam', 'Name': 'Michael', 'Surname': 'Jordan'}
>>>
```

Adding Elements to a Dictionary

Elements inside the dictionary can be added in the same manner that elements are updated in the dictionary.

The only difference is that this time, the key is not present inside the dictionary that we are trying to update. When the key is not present, the key:value gets added inside the dictionary.

```
dict_1 = {1: 'Ram', 2: 'Shyam', 'Name':'Mohan','Surname':'Sharma'}

print('Original dict_1 dictionary: ',dict_1)

# Adding the value as the key Subject is not present in dictionary
dict_1['Subject'] = 'Python'

print('Updated dict_1 dictionary: ',dict_1)
```

Output

```
Original dict_1 dictionary:  {1: 'Ram', 2: 'Shyam', 'Name': 'Mohan', 'Surname': 'Sharma'}
Updated dict_1 dictionary:  {1: 'Ram', 2: 'Shyam', 'Name': 'Mohan', 'Surname': 'Sharma', 'Subject': 'Python'}
>>>
```

Removing Elements From the Dictionary

- **Using the del keyword**
  We can use the del keyword to remove specific items or the entire dictionary itself from the dictionary.
- **Using the pop() method**
  We can use the pop() method to remove a particular item from the dictionary. We can pass the key inside the pop() method to remove that key-value pair from the dictionary. Also, it returns the value that is being removed.

- **Using the popitem() method**

  The popitem() method can be used to remove an arbitrary key:value pair from the dictionary.
- **Using the clear() method**

  If we want to make a dictionary empty, we can use the clear() method, which removes all the key:value pairs from the dictionary.

Given below is a code snippet that uses all these methods to remove items from the dictionary:

```python
dict_1 = {1:'Ram',2:'Shyam',3:'Balram',4:'Sam',5:'Rohit',
          6:'Mohit',7:'Danny',8:'Jordan',9:'Michael',10:'Sumit',11:'Suraj'}

print('Original dict_1 dictionary: ',dict_1)

# Using del keyword to remove Sam from the dictionary
del dict_1[4]
print('\nUpdated dict_1 dictionary after removing Sam using del method is: ',dict_1)

# Using pop() method to remove specifically Mohit from the dictionary
removed_item = dict_1.pop(6)
print('\nRemoved item using pop() method is: ',removed_item)
print('\nUpdated dict_1 dictionary after removal is: ',dict_1)

# Using popitem() method to remove an arbitrary element from the dictionary
popped_item = dict_1.popitem()
print('\npopped item from the popitem() method is: ',popped_item)
print('\nUpdated dict_1 dictionary after removal is: ',dict_1)

# Using clear() method to remove all the elements from the dictionary
dict_1.clear()
print('\nUpdated dict_1 dictionary after using clear() method is: ',dict_1)
```

Upon executing the above source code, we will get the following Output

```
= RESTART: C:\Users\Saurabh Gupta\AppData\Local\Programs\Python\Python39\if.py =
Original dict_1 dictionary:  {1: 'Ram', 2: 'Shyam', 3: 'Balram', 4: 'Sam', 5: 'Rohit', 6: 'Mohit', 7: 'Danny', 8: 'Jordan
', 9: 'Michael', 10: 'Sumit', 11: 'Suraj'}

Updated dict_1 dictionary after removing Sam using del method is:  {1: 'Ram', 2: 'Shyam', 3: 'Balram', 5: 'Rohit', 6: 'Mo
hit', 7: 'Danny', 8: 'Jordan', 9: 'Michael', 10: 'Sumit', 11: 'Suraj'}

Removed item using pop() method is:  Mohit

Updated dict_1 dictionary after removal is:  {1: 'Ram', 2: 'Shyam', 3: 'Balram', 5: 'Rohit', 7: 'Danny', 8: 'Jordan', 9:
'Michael', 10: 'Sumit', 11: 'Suraj'}

popped item from the popitem() method is:  (11, 'Suraj')

Updated dict_1 dictionary after removal is:  {1: 'Ram', 2: 'Shyam', 3: 'Balram', 5: 'Rohit', 7: 'Danny', 8: 'Jordan', 9:
'Michael', 10: 'Sumit'}

Updated dict_1 dictionary after using clear() method is:  {}
>>> |
```

Built-In Function and Methods of Dictionary

A few built-in functions are used along with dictionaries to get certain outputs that are discussed in the table below:

Function Name	Description
len(dictionary)	It returns the total number of elements present inside a dictionary.
cmp(dict1,dict2)	These are used to compare two dictionaries.
all()	It returns a True value if all the elements present inside the dictionary are True or if the dictionary is empty.
any()	It returns a True value if any of the elements present inside the dictionary is True. If the dictionary is empty, it will return False.
sorted()	It returns a sorted list of keys in the dictionary.

Dictionary also supports multiple methods that are used for performing different actions. Some of the most commonly used methods are discussed below:

Method Name	Syntax	Description
clear()	dict.clear()	It removes all the elements from the dictionary.
has_key()	dict.has_key(key)	It inserts a True value when that key is present inside the dictionary. Otherwise, it returns False.
items()	dict.items()	It returns a list of dictionary's key-value pairs in the form of tuples.
keys()	dict.keys()	It returns a list of dictionary keys.
values()	dict.values()	It returns a list of all the values present inside a dictionary.
update()	dict.update(dict2)	It adds the elements present inside the dict2 dictionary in the dict dictionary.
copy()	dict.copy()	It returns a shallow copy of the dictionary dict.

An Appeal from the Publisher

Hello wonderful reader!

We hope you are enjoying this book.

We wanted to let you know that you have made an impact on many lives by reading this book.

Just to give you a brief introduction: We are a small publishing company with a team of 8 writers and 2 editors.

Most of our employees come from financially weaker section and our company is the only means they support their families. This is our way of giving back to the society.

We don't have the giant advertising budgets that many other publishers and businesses do online.

So, one way that you can really support our mission and our business is by leaving us a review on this book.

For a small company like us, getting reviews (especially on Amazon) means we can submit our books for advertising.

This means we can actually sell a few copies from time to time and make a bigger impact on the society as a whole. So, every review means a lot to us.

We can't THANK YOU enough for this!

UNDERSTANDING FUNCTIONS

Functions

Functions in Python are a block of code that encloses within itself a series of code/statements used to perform a single/related action. A function helps us provide modularity to our source program. It helps us with code reusability and data abstraction. The block can be called multiple times and executed from anywhere in the programs once it gets declared.

Two types of functions that exist in Python are:

i.   Built-in functions

Those functions that are already declared inside Python and are available for usage by the users are called built-in functions. Up to now, we have come across many such functions, like print(), id(), len(), list(), etc. All these are simply built-in functions. We do not need to know about the internal code structure; we can use it directly as per our requirements.

ii.   User-defined functions

But wait a second; is that it? Have you ever wondered what to do if you must perform a certain set of actions multiple times, but their functionality is not provided beforehand by Python? Then what will

you do? Writing the same piece of code again and again will result in an unorganized code structure and will pose serious trouble when it comes to the debugging part of the program. Thus, to resolve this issue, Python provides us with a feature to write our user-defined functions.

Defining a Function

To define a function, we must follow proper syntax and some rules that are discussed below:

- We must use the def keyword along with the name of the function to define a function.
- The arguments that we want to pass within a function must be placed inside parentheses ().
- Just like loops and conditional expressions, here we also use the semicolon (:) delimiter to mark the start of the function.
- The function body is written inside an intended block (4 spaces are used for indentation).
- The first statement that we write inside a function is a docstring that explains the working of the function, i.e., what the function is supposed to do. Writing a docstring is optional.
- We can exit the statement with a return statement. The return keyword passes a value back to the caller. It is also optional as to whether or not we want to return any value.

Syntax

def function_name(params/args)
''' A docstring specifying functionality of code '''
statement(s)

Making a Call to the Function

We can make a call to the function by using its name followed by the parenthesis symbols. Note that we must declare the function before we make a call to it. If the function declaration is not found, the interpreter gives an error. We can make a function call from anywhere in the source code.

Let's look at an example to understand how we can make custom functions ourselves. We will be creating a custom function to print the 'Hello World' string as an output. Take a look at the following code snippet.

```python
def hello():
    '''This function prints Hello World string when called.'''

    print('Hello World')

# Function ends when we move out of the intended block

print('Output obtained after calling the hello() function first time')
# Making a function call
hello()

print('Output obtained after calling the hello() function second time')
hello()
```

When we run and execute the code, you will notice that whenever we make a call to the hello() function, the 'Hello World' string gets printed as the output on the console.

```
= RESTART: C:\Users\Saurabh Gupta\AppData\Local\Programs\Python\Python39\if.py
Output obtained after calling the hello() function first time
Hello World
Output obtained after calling the hello() function second time
Hello World
>>>
```

Return Statement

The return statement represents the end of the function block and sends the control back to the place from where the function was being called. The statement associated with the return keyword gets evaluated and its value is returned by the function. If we don't want to return any statement, writing the return statement is optional. In this case, the function itself returns a None-type object.

```python
def polarity(num):
    '''This function tells whether a number is
    positive or negative'''

    if num >= 0:
        return 'It is positive'
    else:
        return 'It is negative'


print(polarity(10))

print(polarity(-10))
```

The output of the above code snippet will be shown as follows:

```
= RESTART: C:\Users\Saurabh Gupta\AppData\Local\Programs\Python\Python39\if.py =
It is positive
It is negative
>>>
```

Types of Arguments

We can pass several different types of arguments inside a function at the time of function call. These arguments are:

i.   Default arguments

When we do not pass any value to an argument inside a function, the interpreter assumes a default value of that argument by itself. These arguments are termed default arguments. The following code snippet will give you a much better understanding of the same.

```
def personal_info( name, age = 35 ):
    "This prints a passed info into this function"
    print("Name of the boy is : ", name)
    print("His Age : ", age)

# Making a call to personal_info function with both arguments

personal_info( name="Rahul", age=25)

# Making a call to personal_info function with only one argument
personal_info( name="Rahul" )
```

In the code, we have first created a custom function called personal_info() that accepts two arguments: name and age. Age argument is our default argument here, as it already consists of a value equal to 35. When we call the function by passing both the arguments

explicitly, the arguments passed will be copied and used inside the function. However, when we pass only the name and not the age, the interpreter implicitly assumes the argument value as the default one which was given during declaration. Thus, age is our default argument here.

```
= RESTART: C:\Users\Saurabh Gupta\AppData\Local\Programs\Python\Python39\if.py =
Name of the boy is :   Rahul
His Age :   25
Name of the boy is :   Rahul
His Age :   35
>>>
```

ii.   Required arguments

A few arguments must be passed while we are making a call to the function. These arguments are called required arguments. In required arguments, one should note that the arguments passed during the function call should match exactly in terms of order with the positions of the arguments in the function declaration. If the order doesn't match, or if the argument count is less, it will throw an error.

```
def personal_info(name, surname, gender, age):

    '''This function prints passed personal information of a boy'''

    print("Name of the boy is : ", name)
    print("Name of the boy is : ", surname)
    print("Gender : ", gender)
    print("His Age : ", age)


# Making a call to personal_info function with required arguments

# Arguments passed during function call needs to be in same order as in function declaration
personal_info('Rahul','Sharma','Male',25)
```

The output of the following code upon execution will be given as:

```
= RESTART: C:\Users\Saurabh Gupta\AppData\Local\Programs\Python\Python39\if.py =
Name of the boy is :   Rahul
Name of the boy is :   Sharma
Gender :   Male
His Age :   25
>>>
```

iii. Keyword arguments

When we do not want to remember the order of arguments, we can use the keyword arguments. The benefit of using the keyword argument is that it remembers the argument values by the keyword given during the declaration of the function.

The following code snippet will give you a better understanding of the same.

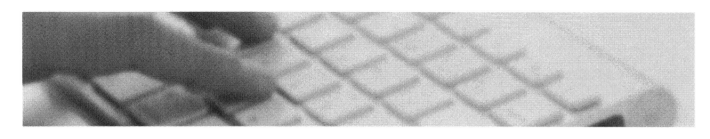

```
def personal_info(name, surname, gender, age):

    '''This function prints passed personal information of a boy'''
    print("Name of the boy is : ", name)
    print("Surname of the boy is : ", surname)
    print("Gender : ", gender)
    print("His age : ", age)

# Making a call to personal_info function with keyword arguments

# Arguments passed during function call need not be in same order as function declaration
personal_info(age = 25, name='Rahul', gender='Male', surname='Sharma')

|
```

The output of the following code upon execution will be given as:

```
= RESTART: C:\Users\Saurabh Gupta\AppData\Local\Programs\Python\Python39\if.py
Name of the boy is :  Rahul
Surname of the boy is :  Sharma
Gender :  Male
His age :  25
>>> |
```

We can notice that though the parameters are not in the same order as in the function declaration, the function can recognize the parameters with the help of keywords used in the arguments passed during the function call.

iv. Variable-length arguments

Sometimes we may not know the number of arguments that we will require in the project when defining a function. For such cases, we can use variable-length arguments. In this, we pass comma-separated values that are internally treated as tuples during the function call. These tuples can be used to pass any number of arguments inside a function during a function call.

For declaring variable-length arguments, we follow the syntax *args. Take a look at the following example:

```python
def personal_info(*args):

    '''This function prints passed personal information of a boy'''
    for i in args:
        print(i)


# Making a call to personal_info function with variable-length arguments

# Arguments passed during function call using comma separated values
personal_info('Rahul','Sharma','Male',25)
```

```
>>>
= RESTART: C:\Users\Saurabh Gupta\AppData\Local\Programs\Python\Python39\if.py =
Rahul
Sharma
Male
25
>>>
```

Scope and Lifetime of a Variable

Once declared in a program, variables may not be accessible at each place in the program. The accessibility of the variable depends largely on the location where the variable is declared. The scope of a variable is the part of the program where that variable can be accessed inside the program. Similarly, the term 'lifetime of a variable' refers to the period up to which the variable remains present in the memory after getting declared.

We can classify variables into two categories based on their scope: global variables and local variables.

- **Global variables:** Those variables that, upon declaration, remain accessible throughout the program are called global variables.
- **Local variables:** These variables are accessible within a function only. As soon as we move inside the function body, local variables come into the scope. As we move out of the function body, the local variable gets destroyed and its value becomes unrecognized when we again call the function.

Let's take a look at an example through which we can observe the difference in the workings of local and global variables.

```
def scope():
    ''' local variable declaration'''
    var = 10
    print("Value of local var variable inside function:",var)

# declaring a global variable named var
var = 100

# calling the user-defined scope() function
scope()

print("Value of global var variable outside function:",var)

```

The output of the above-given source code will be shown as:

```
>>>
= RESTART: C:\Users\Saurabh Gupta\AppData\Local\Programs\Python\Python39\if.py =
Value of local var variable inside function: 10
Value of global var variable outside function: 100
>>>
```

When we save and execute the program we can observe, we first assign the value of var variable as 100 globally. Then, we make a call to the scope() function. Inside the scope function, we declare a local var variable and assign a value of 10 to it. As soon as the local variable is assigned, it comes into the scope of the function. When we print the value of the variable, it recognizes the local variable and prints its value as 10.

Now, as soon as the function block ends, the scope of the local variable from the memory gets destroyed and is no longer recognized by the interpreter, so when we print the value of the variable outside the function, 100 gets printed as a global variable assigned a value of 100.

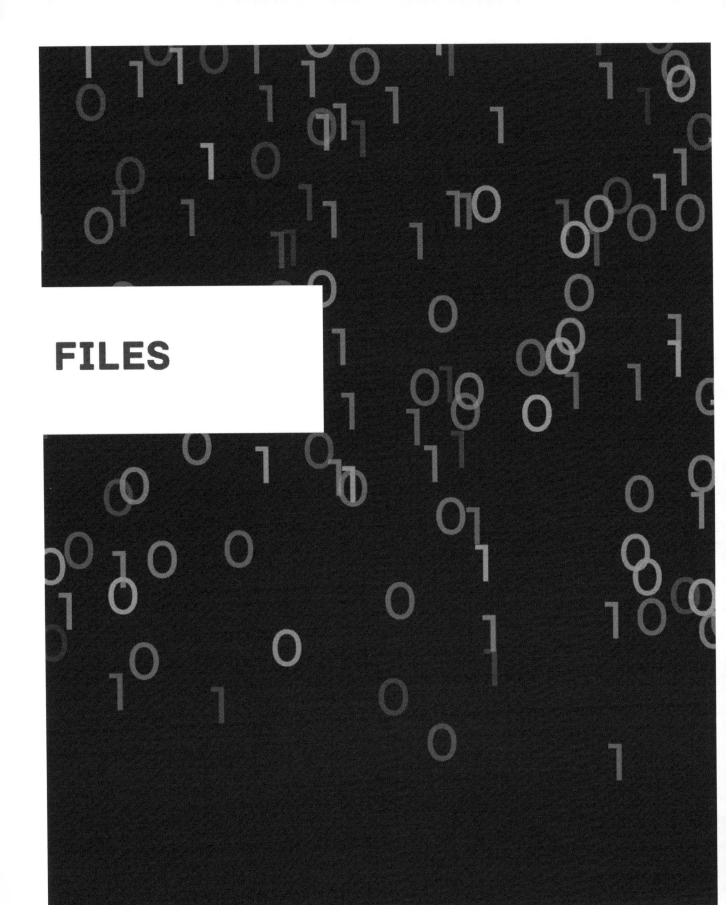

FILES

Files

We cannot always place our data into source code and read it using the interpreter. Source codes are volatile and can be changed. To resolve this problem, we use files that are non-volatile and can be stored on our secondary storage devices such as a hard disk. Like many other programming languages, Python offers the freedom to manipulate these files stored on our system using some predefined built-in functions.

These functions can be used to perform different operations on a file like opening, closing, editing, etc. We carry out manipulation in the files using a file object (we will see later in the chapter). Python gives us the freedom to handle both binary files and text files. Python treats these files differently. In Python, the interpreter looks out for an end-of-line (EOL) character like a comma (,) or a new line character (\n) at the end of each line. This helps the interpreter understand that the existing line has ended and a new line has begun. Let's proceed and understand how we can work with files in Python.

Opening a File

To manipulate a file, we first need to open it from our secondary storage devices. For this, we use the built-in open() function. This function opens a file and returns a file object, which will be further used to perform manipulative operations on the file.

The syntax of the open() function is given as:
file_obj = **open**(file [, access_mode][, buffer_value])

The open() method accepts three parameters. These are explained below:

- **file**: This is the name of the file that we want to open.
- **access_mode:** This is an optional parameter that specifies in which mode we want to open the file. It could be any of read, write, append, etc. A full list of different access modes available in Python is given in a tabular form below.
- **buffer_value:** This defines the desired buffer size of the files in memory. When the buffer_value is set to 0, buffering will not take place. When it is 1, a line is buffered into the memory. When we set any positive value greater than 1, we get the buffer size of that input in the value. When it is less than 0, the buffer size is set to the system's default value.

Different file opening modes along with their symbol and description are given in the table below:

Symbol	Description
r	It is the default mode that is used to read a file. It sets the file pointer at the beginning of the file for reading.
w	It is used to open a file for writing purposes only. If the file already exists in the system then it opens and overwrites the content on the file otherwise if a file is not present it creates a new file.
x	It opens a file for exclusive creation, if the file already exists in the system then this operation fails.
A	It can be used for appending into a file. It sets the file pointer to the end of the existing file so that the file can be appended. If a pre-existing file is not found then it creates a new file for writing.
rb	It is same as the read mode but instead it opens the file in binary format. File pointer is set at the beginning of the file when it starts reading the binary file.
wb	It opens the file for writing in binary format. If the file already exists in the system then it opens and overwrites the content on the file otherwise if a file is not present it creates a new file.
ab	It can be used for appending into a file in binary format. It sets the file pointer to the end of the file so that the file can be appended. If a pre-existing file is not found then it creates a new file for appending and writing.
r+	In this mode, we can open the file for both reading and writing at the same time.
w+	It is used to open a file for both writing and reading. If the file already exists in the system then it opens and overwrites the content on the file otherwise if a file is not present it creates a new file for writing and reading.
a+	It is used to open a file for both appending and reading. If the file already exists in the system then the file pointer is set at the end of the file for appending and reading and if the file is not present it creates a new file for appending and reading.
rb+	It opens the file for reading and writing in binary format. . The file pointer is set at the beginning of the file when it starts reading or writing the binary file.
wb+	It opens the file for writing and reading in binary format. If the file already exists in the system then it opens and overwrites the content on the file otherwise if a file is not present it creates a new file.
ab+	It can be used for both appending and reading into a file in binary format. It sets the file pointer to the end of the file so that the file can be appended. If a pre-existing file is not found then it creates a new file for appending and reading.

Note: When we give the name of the file as a parameter inside the open() function, the file must be stored in the same location from where the interpreter is getting loaded, or we should provide the entire absolute path of the file along with the file name. This will let the interpreter know from which location it must read the file. If it fails to read the file, it will throw a filenotfound error.

Closing Files in Python

After completing the desired operations over a file, we must close it because this frees up the resources of our system acquired during the opening of the file. This is done with the help of a built-in close() function. Although Python has a garbage collector that cleans up unreferenced objects, we should not remain dependent on it and must close the file using the close() method. It is always a good coding practice to do so.

The syntax of the close() function is given as:
file_obj.close(), where file_obj is the referenced file object created after opening a file.

Different Attributes of a File Object

The file object comes with a variety of attributes that can be used to get various information related to the file. Some of the attributes are:

- **file_obj.name:** This tells the name of the file that is opened using the particular file object.
- **file_obj.mode:** This tells the mode in which the file is opened.
- **file_obj.closed:** This returns a True value when the file object is closed; otherwise, it returns False.
- **file_obj.softspace:** This returns a True value when a space character is explicitly required to be printed before another value when we use a print statement. Otherwise, it returns False.

Let's see an example of how we can open and close a file, as well as the usage of some of the file object attributes:

```
file_obj = open('file1.txt','r')

# Checking if file is opened or closed
print('Is file closed?', file_obj.closed)

# Printing name of the open file
print('Name of the open file is: ',file_obj.name)

# Printing mode in which the file is opened
print('Mode of opening the file is: ',file_obj.mode)

# Closing the file
file_obj.close()

# Rechecking if file is opened or closed
print('Is file closed now?', file_obj.closed)
```

When we save and execute the above-written source code, we will get the following Output

```
= RESTART: C:\Users\Saurabh Gupta\AppData\Local\Programs\Python\Python39\if.py
Is file closed? False
Name of the open file is:  file1.txt
Mode of opening the file is:  r
Is file closed now? True
>>> |
```

Although we can close a file using the close() method and file object, there can be a situation in which this function may not work properly. When we open a file using the open() method and perform some action using the file object, suppose some exception occurs while we are performing the operations. Then the close() method statement written at the bottom of the source code will not execute; the code will exit with closing the file and the resources of the system will remain occupied.

To overcome this ambiguous condition, we use the with statement that provides a guarantee that the close() method will automatically get executed as we move out of the with statement block. In this case, we need not write the close() method separately.

Take a look at the following code snippet:

```
with open ('file1.txt','r') as file_obj:
    # Intended block marks start of the with block

    # Checking if file is opened or closed
    print('Is file closed?', file_obj.closed)

    # Printing name of the open file
    print('Name of the open file is: ',file_obj.name)

    # Printing mode in which the file is opened
    print('Mode of opening the file is: ',file_obj.mode)

# As we move out of intended block file automatically closes
# Rechecking if file is opened or closed
print('Is file closed now?', file_obj.closed)
```

When we save and execute the above-written source code, we will get the following Output

```
= RESTART: C:\Users\Saurabh Gupta\AppData\Local\Programs\Python\Python39\if.py
Is file closed? False
Name of the open file is:  file1.txt
Mode of opening the file is:  r
Is file closed now? True
>>> |
```

Reading a File in Python

As discussed above, to read a file in Python, we must open that file in read mode.

- **read() method**

  To read a file, we can use the read() method. The syntax of the read() method is given as:

  file_obj.read([value])

  This method accepts one parameter value that denotes the number of bytes that we want to read from the beginning of the opened file. If we do not pass any value as a parameter, it reads as much data as it can and goes on to read until it reaches the end of the file. Upon reaching the end of the file, it generates a '\n' new line character. Suppose we have a file named file1.txt, having content as shown in the following image:

  file1.txt - Notepad

  File Edit Format View Help

  The Taj Mahal is a historic and the most beautiful place in the world.
  The cultural monument is located in Agra, Uttar Pradesh, India, and holds a symbol of love.
  This seamless beauty is constructed using white marbles and is a hotspot of tourist attraction.
  The Mughal Architecture represents cultural diversity prevailing in the country and is identified as UNESCO World Heritage Site the year 2007.
  Below this historic paradise lies the tombs of great Indian kings and queens cremated in the darkroom.

  The great Rabindranath Tagore refers to the Taj Mahal as " the dream of marble."
  Located on the banks of the river Yamuna, the green atmosphere surrounding the monument increases the fragrance of the environment.
  The monument's view gets brightened by the beautiful moonlight dawned at night.

We want to read the content written inside this file. It can be done as:

```
with open ('file1.txt','r') as file_obj:

    # we are reading and printing first 13 bytes of data from the file
    print(file_obj.read(13))

# Rechecking if file is opened or closed after exiting the with block
print('\nIs file closed now?', file_obj.closed)

# Reopening the file again
with open ('file1.txt','r') as obj:

    # We are not passing any value inside the read() method, so it will read till the last
    print(obj.read())

# Rechecking if file is opened or closed after exiting the with block
print('\nIs file closed now?', obj.closed)

```

The output of the source code after saving and executing the file will get generated as:

```
= RESTART: C:\Users\Saurabh Gupta\AppData\Local\Programs\Python\Python39\if.py =
>>>
The Taj Mahal

Is file closed now? True
The Taj Mahal is a historic and the most beautiful place in the world.
The cultural monument is located in Agra, Uttar Pradesh, India, and holds a symbol of love.
This seamless beauty is constructed using white marbles and is a hotspot of tourist attraction.
The Mughal Architecture represents cultural diversity prevailing in the country and is identified as UNESCO World Heritag
e Site the year 2007.
Below this historic paradise lies the tombs of great Indian kings and queens cremated in the darkroom.

The great Rabindranath Tagore refers to the Taj Mahal as " the dream of marble."
Located on the banks of the river Yamuna, the green atmosphere surrounding the monument increases the fragrance of the en
vironment.
The monument's view gets brightened by the beautiful moonlight dawned at night.

Is file closed now? True
>>>
```

- **readline() method**

  To read a file line by line until a newline character is reached, we use the readline() method.

  We can see, in the following image, how the readline() method prints text inside the file line by line each time we call it.

```
Type "help", "copyright", "credits" or "license()" for more information.
>>> file_obj = open('file1.txt','r')
>>> file_obj.readline()
'The Taj Mahal is a historic and the most beautiful place in the world.\n'
>>> file_obj.readline()
'The cultural monument is located in Agra, Uttar Pradesh, India, and holds a symbol of love.\n'
>>> file_obj.readline()
'This seamless beauty is constructed using white marbles and is a hotspot of tourist attraction.\n'
>>> file_obj.readline()
'The Mughal Architecture represents cultural diversity prevailing in the country and is identified as UNESCO World Herita
ge Site the year 2007.\n'
>>> file_obj.readline()
'Below this historic paradise lies the tombs of great Indian kings and queens cremated in the darkroom.\n'
>>> |
```

- **readlines() method**

  The readlines() method is used to return a list of all possible lines in a file. See the code and its output below.

```
>>> file_obj.readlines()
['The Taj Mahal is a historic and the most beautiful place in the world.\n', 'The cultural monument is located in Agra, U
ttar Pradesh, India, and holds a symbol of love.\n', 'This seamless beauty is constructed using white marbles and is a ho
tspot of tourist attraction.\n', 'The Mughal Architecture represents cultural diversity prevailing in the country and is
identified as UNESCO World Heritage Site the year 2007.\n', 'Below this historic paradise lies the tombs of great Indian
kings and queens cremated in the darkroom.\n', '\n', 'The great Rabindranath Tagore refers to the Taj Mahal as " the drea
m of marble."\n', 'Located on the banks of the river Yamuna, the green atmosphere surrounding the monument increases the
fragrance of the environment.\n', 'The monument's view gets brightened by the beautiful moonlight dawned at night.']
>>> |
```

Writing to a File in Python

We can write to a file by opening it in either append mode (a), exclusive creation (x) mode, or write mode (w).

Note that when a file is not present inside the memory and then we try to open it using write (w) mode or append (a) mode, a new file is automatically created. If the file exists, opening it in write (w) mode will overwrite the existing content in the file. Let us take a look at an example in which we will be using the built-in write() method to write in a file.

```python
with open ('file2.txt','w') as file_obj:

    # we are writing the string inside the file
    file_obj.write('This is the content I want to add inside new file.')

# Reopening the file again and reading the content inside it
with open ('file2.txt','r') as obj:

    # We are not passing any value inside the read() method, so it will read till the last
    print(obj.read())
```

We are first opening a file with the name 'file2.txt'. As it doesn't exist in the system, a new file with that name will automatically be created. Then we will pass the string inside the write() method that we want to add inside out file. As we exit the first with block, the file will automatically get closed; then we will reopen it in read mode and verify what content is written inside the file. When we save and execute the

source code, the output will be printed as the content we added to our file.

```
>>>
= RESTART: C:\Users\Saurabh Gupta\AppData\Local\Programs\Python\Python39\if.py =
This is the content I want to add inside new file.
>>> |
```

We can also verify it by opening the created file on our system and checking whether or not the content is added. A file with the name 'file2.txt' will be added to the system.

```
file2 - Notepad
File  Edit  Format  View  Help
This is the content I want to add inside new file.
```

Additional File Object Methods

Several file object methods exist. These are listed below along with their description.

Method	Description
file_obj.read(value)	It is used to read data from a file maximum up to the value passed. If the value is not passed or if it is negative, it reads until the end of the file is reached.
file_obj.readline(value)	It is used to read and return one line from a file. If the value is specified, it reads up to that place only.
file_obj.readlines(value)	It reads and returns a list of all possible lines inside a file. If the value is specified, it reads up to that place only.
file_obj.readable()	This method returns True if the file is readable. Otherwise, it returns False.
file_obj.write(string)	It writes the passed string inside a file.
file_obj.writelines(lines)	It writes a sequence of lines inside the file. Generally, a list is passed.
file_obj.writable()	This method returns True if the file can be written. Otherwise, it returns False.

Method	Description
file_obj.seek(offset,from)	It changes the location of the file pointer to offset bytes with reference to from (start, current, end) position.
file_obj.tell()	It returns the current location of the file pointer inside the file.
file_obj.truncate()	It is used to resize the file stream.
file_obj.seekable()	It returns True if the file stream can be accessed randomly. Otherwise, it returns False.
file_obj.close()	It is used to close the opened file stream.
file_obj.flush()	It is used to flush the write buffer of the file stream.
file_obj.isatty()	It returns a True value if the file stream used is interactive. Otherwise, it returns False.

MODULES, PACKAGES, AND EXCEPTION HANDLING

Modules

Modules in Python are actually Python program files that are created to increase the reusability of code. Modules contain nothing but different functions, classes, variables, etc. that are themselves runnable. In simpler words, the Python source code file that we save using the .py extension can actually be used as a module. The modules allow a programmer to logically organize our Python code.

Suppose that we have some functions that we use regularly, but every time we start writing a program, we implement it from scratch. In such cases, we can save those common functions inside a Python file (so that it becomes a module), and then we can use them directly inside other programs that will perform all the functions that exist inside the module file without having to write all the functions from scratch.

Python already consists of a standard library of modules inside which many functions are already present that we directly use. These files automatically get stored inside the Lib directory at the location where Python is installed on our system.

Loading One Python Module Into Another Python File

Now comes the question of how we can load one Python file (module) into another Python file. This task of importing files is achieved with the help of two statements in Python that are listed below. We will discuss them in a bit more detail.

- The **import** statement
  The import statement can be used to import all the functionalities of one Python file into another Python file. Whenever the Python interpreter finds the import statement written in a file, it looks for that module file inside the search path. A search path is a list of all the directories inside which the interpreter searches for that particular module for importing. Usually, whenever we try to import one module into another, we may give the path ourselves, or both files should be stored in the same folder.

For locating a module, this sequence is followed:
- First, the present working directory.
- If it is unavailable in the present working directory, it looks for modules in the PYTHONPATH shell variable. (Recall that we read about this shell variable in chapter 2.)
- If it is still unavailable, the default path is checked.

The search path is located inside the system module as a sys.path variable. The sys.path variable contains everything present in the working directory, PYTHONPATH, and the installation-dependent default path.

Let's create a user-defined module ourselves and try importing its functionalities into another Python code.
We will write a module named file1.py and try to import it into another file named file2.py. See the images given below:
The content of file1.py in which we have written two user-defined functions that will be imported in file2 and will get executed.

```python
# First Python file which will act as module


# Creating a general function that returns a string
def greet_user():
        print('Hello User !! function greet_user invoked successfully')
        print('This function is located in file1 module')
        print('You imported it successfully')


# Creating a function that prints cube of a number passed inside it
def print_cube(num):
        print('function print_cube invoked successfully')
        print('This function is located in file1 module')
        print('Cube of the number is: ', num**3)
        print('You imported it successfully')
```

The content of file2.py in which we import file1 and call the functions defined in the file1.py module using the (.) notation.

```
# importing the module file1

import file1

# Making a call to the greet_user() function located in the file1 module
file1.greet_user()


# Making a call to the print_cube() function located in the file1 module
file1.print_cube(5)
```

When we save and run the **file2.py** file, functions defined inside the **file1** module will also get executed as we imported them in the **file2.py** file.

```
= RESTART: C:\Users\Saurabh Gupta\AppData\Local\Programs\Python\Python39\file2.p
y
Hello User !! function greet_user invoked successfully
This function is located in file1 module
You imported it successfully
function print_cube invoked successfully
This function is located in file1 module
Cube of the number is:  125
You imported it successfully
>>>
```

- The **from-import** statement

  The from-import statement can be used to import specific functions from a particular module. Its syntax is written as:

  from module_name import function_name

  We can even import all the functions inside the module using the regex expression (*) that refers to all. Then we will use the syntax like:

  from module_name import *

  Let's see our previous example but this time we will call only the print_cube() function specifically in our file2.py file.

```
# importing the module file1

from file1 import print_cube


# Making a call to the print_cube() function located in the file1 module
print_cube(10)

|
```

The output of file2.py after executing the above-written source code will be shown as:

```
= RESTART: C:\Users\Saurabh Gupta\AppData\Local\Programs\Python\Python39\file2.p
y
function print_cube invoked successfully
This function is located in file1 module
Cube of the number is:  1000
You imported it successfully
>>>
```

The dir() Function

The dir() is an in-built function used to return the list of all the functions, variables, and modules inside a particular module. The returned list is sorted. Let's import the math module in Python, apply the dir() function, and observe its output.

```python
import math

print(dir(math))
```

When the program runs, the output will be generated as given below. The sorted list contains all the functions, variables, classes, etc. present inside the math module.

```
= RESTART: C:\Users\Saurabh Gupta\AppData\Local\Programs\Python\Python39\if.py =
['__doc__', '__loader__', '__name__', '__package__', '__spec__', 'acos', 'acosh', 'asin', 'asinh', 'atan', 'atan2', 'atan
h', 'ceil', 'comb', 'copysign', 'cos', 'cosh', 'degrees', 'dist', 'e', 'erf', 'erfc', 'exp', 'expm1', 'fabs', 'factorial'
, 'floor', 'fmod', 'frexp', 'fsum', 'gamma', 'gcd', 'hypot', 'inf', 'isclose', 'isfinite', 'isinf', 'isnan', 'isqrt', 'lc
m', 'ldexp', 'lgamma', 'log', 'log10', 'log1p', 'log2', 'modf', 'nan', 'nextafter', 'perm', 'pi', 'pow', 'prod', 'radians
', 'remainder', 'sin', 'sinh', 'sqrt', 'tan', 'tanh', 'tau', 'trunc', 'ulp']
>>> |
```

Packages in Python

A package is an organized, well-structured hierarchy of directories used to store similar modules together inside a single package. A package may contain sub-packages, modules, sub-modules, etc. under it. A directory must contain a special file named __init__.py so that the interpreter could identify it as a package. The __init__.py file holds the import statement of all the sub-packages, modules, and sub-modules inside it.

When we want to create a custom package of our own, we must first create a directory named package in your system from where Python is running. Inside the directory, place the modules and sub-modules that you want to import and later, inside the directory, make a __init__.py file containing all the import statements for modules and sub-modules. Thus, whenever we import this package directory, all of the sub-packages, modules, and sub-modules will get imported automatically.

Errors in Python

While we write programs, we may make mistakes such as typos, wrong logic, missing brackets and colons, etc. All these types of mistakes can lead to an error in the program execution and the program is suddenly terminated. Based on the nature of errors, we can further divide them into two sections:

- **Syntax error**

  When a Python program is written, each statement needs to follow proper syntax. If the proper structure (syntax) is not followed, the syntax errors/parsing errors are bound to happen. These errors occur at the compile time. Let's try to understand it more clearly with the help of an example:

```
>>> def syntax():
            i = 10

            if (i == 10):
            print(numbers mathch with each other)
syntax()
SyntaxError: expected an indented block
```

  In the above-given code snippet, we can notice that the print() statement is flashed to be having a syntax error because after the if statement, the interpreter looks for an indented block that marks

the beginning of the if block. Hence, a syntax error is raised in this case.

- **Logical error (exceptions)**

  The errors that get raised because of mistakes inside the program logic are called logical errors/exceptions. These occur at the run time, after the syntax was already checked for correctness by the interpreter. These exceptions may cause our program to behave differently and may not yield results as per our requirement. It can also change the normal flow of execution of the program. Let's see an example of a logical error:

  Suppose we want to divide a number by 0. We all know that division by 0 is not possible, so the interpreter will raise a ZeroDivisionError exception in the output

  ```
  >>> a = (100 / 0)
  Traceback (most recent call last):
    File "<pyshell#3>", line 1, in <module>
      a = (100 / 0)
  ZeroDivisionError: division by zero
  >>>
  ```

  Similar to this exception many other built-in exceptions exist inside the Exception base class in Python. These are given in the table below along with their description.

Exception	Description
AssertionError	This exception is raised when the assert statement in the program fails to execute.
AttributeError	This exception is raised when the attribute referencing or assignment fails.
EOFError	This is raised when the input() function while performing operations reaches the end of the file.
FloatingPointError	This exception is raised when any floating point operation inside a program fails.
GeneratorExit	This is raised when the close() method of a generator function is invoked.
ImportError	This is raised when we want to import a module and it is not found in the path.
IndexError	This is raised when the index we are searching for is not found inside the sequence.
KeyError	This is raised when the particular key is not available in the memory.
KeyboardInterrupt	This is raised when the programmer on his/her own interrupts the program during its execution using Ctrl+C or the Delete button.
MemoryError	This is raised when, during performing, any operation memory limit is exceeded and the program runs out of memory.
NameError	This exception is raised when we want to access an identifier that is not available in the local or global scope of the program.
NotImplementedError	This exception is raised when an abstract function that must be implemented inside an inherited class does not get implemented.
OSError	This is raised in case of system-related errors.

Exception	Description
OverflowError	This is raised when, during an arithmetic operation, the result crosses the maximum size limit specified for a numeric type and it can't be represented.
RuntimeError	This is raised when the error does not fall under any of the other exception categories.
StopIteration	This is raised when the next() method of a generator does not have any object to point to inside a generator object.
SyntaxError	This is raised in the case of syntax error in the code.
IndentationError	This is raised if an indentation mismatch happens.
TabError	This is raised if there is inconsistent space due to a mismatch of tabs and spaces.
SystemError	This is raised when the interpreter finds some internal error but the interpreter does not get an exit.
SystemExit	This is raised when a Python interpreter automatically gets exited by the sys.exit() function call.
TypeError	This is raised when any operation is performed on a data type that is not supported on the particular data type.
UnboundLocalError	This is raised when we try to access a local variable inside a function but its value hasn't been assigned yet.
UnicodeError	This is raised when any Unicode-related encoding or decoding error happens inside a program.
ValueError	This exception is raised when an in-built function gets an argument of the appropriate data type but the values supplied are themselves inappropriate.
ZeroDivisionError	This is raised when the second operand inside a division or modulo operation is zero.

Handling Exceptions in Python

Up to now, we have read about different types of exceptions and have gotten to know the situation when these exceptions will be raised. These exceptions can terminate our program execution or may result in wrong results. So, it is really important to handle these exceptions. Python provides us with the freedom to use its exception handling statements, with which we can handle these exceptions. In the next paragraph, we will take a look at the try-except block/statement.

The Try-Except-Else Block

If we want to handle some statements in our program that can raise exceptions, we can do so using the try-except block. The suspicious code is placed inside the try block and the code that handles this exception is placed inside the except block. We can club the try-except block with the else block that will get executed if no exceptions are raised. The

syntax of the try-catch block is given as:
```
try:
        suspicious code statement(s)
except Exception_1:
        execute this block if, exception_1 is raised
```

except Exception_2:

    execute this block if, exception_2 is raised

else:

    execute this block, if no exceptions are raised

Let's look at an example of how we can use this try-except-else block to handle our exceptions.

```
def handle_exceptions(a,b):
    try:
        result = a/b

    except ZeroDivisionError:
        print('Division by 0 is not possible')

    else:
        print('Result obtained is: ',result)
a = int(input('Enter the first number: '))
b = int(input('Enter the second number: '))

# Making a call to the function
handle_exceptions(a,b)
```

We have written a function that accepts two arguments, a and b, which are numbers. Now, one of the numbers gets divided by another number and it returns the value inside the variable 'result'. This code can run into exceptions, so we can put this code inside the **try** block. Now, if the ZeroDivisionErrors occurs, the statement inside the **except** block will work. Otherwise, the statement inside the **else** block will execute.

The output obtained after the program is run twice with different values of arguments a and b is as follows:

```
= RESTART: C:\Users\Saurabh Gupta\AppData\Local\Programs\Python\Python39\if.py =
Enter the first number: 10
Enter the second number: 5
Result obtained is:  2.0
>>>
= RESTART: C:\Users\Saurabh Gupta\AppData\Local\Programs\Python\Python39\if.py =
Enter the first number: 10
Enter the second number: 0
Division by 0 is not possible
>>> |
```

First, we run the program with the numbers 10 and 5, so 10 gets divided by 5 and the result obtained is 2. Hence, no exception is raised and the statement inside the **else** block gets executed.

In the next attempt, we run the program with the numbers 10 and 0. This time, 10 gets divided by 0, which is not possible and the ZeroDivisionError exception is raised. Hence, the statement inside the **except** block got executed.

Thus, using the try-except-else block, we can see that we can handle exceptions efficiently and our program will not terminate or give improper results on its own.

The Try-Except-Else Block With No Exceptions/Multiple Exceptions

We can even write an exception block without the name of the exceptions. This is called an except block with no exceptions. In this, the except block will not wait for a specific exception to get raised; it automatically gets raised if any of the exceptions occurs. However, it is not advisable to use this because it is not considered good coding practice. This is because the programmer will never know what exception occurred, as it gets handled automatically.

Its syntax is given as:

try:
    suspicious code statement(s)
except:
    execute this block if any of the exceptions is raised
else:
    execute this block if no exception is raised

Similarly, we can pass more than one exception in the form of a tuple to the except clause. This is called an except block with multiple statements.

Its syntax will be given as:

```
try:
        suspicious code statement(s)
except (exception_1, exception_2, exception_3, exception_4, ...):
    execute this block if any of the exceptions is raised
else:
        execute this block if no exception is raised
```

The Try-Finally Block

We can club a finally block with the try block. Inside the finally block, we place the code statements that must get executed whether or not an exception is raised by the try block.

The syntax of the try-finally block is given below:

```
try:
        suspicious code statement(s)
except exception_1:
        execute this block if exception_1 is raised
else:
        execute this block if no exception is raised
finally:
        statement(s) that will always get executed
```

Let's look at an example to see it working:

```python
def handle_exceptions(a,b):
    try:
        result = a/b

    except ZeroDivisionError:
        print('Division by 0 is not possible')

    else:
        print('Result obtained is: ',result)

    finally:
        print('Statement inside finally block will always execute.')
a = int(input('Enter the first number: '))
b = int(input('Enter the second number: '))

# Making a call to the function
handle_exceptions(a,b)
```

We just added a finally block to our previous example and we can see in the output whether or not an exception is raised. The statement inside the finally block gets executed. The output of the above-given code is shown below:

```
= RESTART: C:\Users\Saurabh Gupta\AppData\Local\Programs\Python\Python39\if
Enter the first number: 10
Enter the second number: 5
Result obtained is:  2.0
Statement inside finally block will always execute.
>>>
= RESTART: C:\Users\Saurabh Gupta\AppData\Local\Programs\Python\Python39\if
Enter the first number: 10
Enter the second number: 0
Division by 0 is not possible
Statement inside finally block will always execute.
>>>
```

Raising an Exception

We can even raise exceptions on our own using the raise statement. We can pass values with the exception specifying that particular exception got raised. The syntax to be followed for using the raise statement is given below:

raise exception_1 (value)

Let's implement a practical example:

```python
def raise_exception(num):
    try:
        if(num <= 0):
            raise ValueError("The number you entered is negative!")
    except ValueError as e:
        print(e)

num = int(input("Enter a positive number: "))

# Calling the function
raise_exception(num)
```

We take a number as an input and then pass this number inside the raise_exception() function as an argument. The function checks if the number is less than 0. Then it raises the exception in the try block itself using the raise statement that the number passed is negative. We can use the reference variable 'e' to identify what exception occurred. The string that we passed as the value with the raise statement gets printed as the value of reference variable e.

When the code snippet is run, the following output will be obtained:

```
= RESTART: C:\Users\Saurabh Gupta\AppData\Local\Programs\Python\Python39\if.p
Enter a positive number: -1
The number you entered is negative!
>>>
```

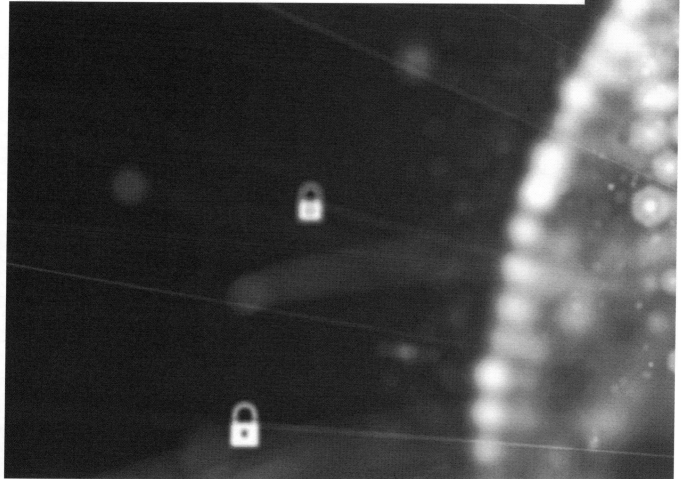

CLASSES, OBJECTS, AND INHERITANCE

Recall that in chapter 1, we discussed a few important features of Python. One of those important features was Python being an object-oriented programming language. Python supports the idea of creating objects for solving problems.

One of the main focuses of OOPs is to increase code reusability. It is based on the concept of DRY (Don't Repeat Yourself). Apart from code reusability, OOP-based programming can be used to provide more security to our data.

In this chapter, we will be reading about the concepts of Classes, Objects, and Inheritance in detail.

Classes in Python

A class is a user-defined data structure that can be considered a blueprint/prototype from which objects are created. Classes can be used to bundle together data and their functionalities. Classes have a set of attributes and methods attached to them. Class attributes are simply the data members such as class variables and instance variables present inside the class, whereas methods are functionalities that are used for modifying the state of these attributes.

The classes can be created by using the class keyword. The syntax for defining a class can be written as:

class Name_of_class:

  …………………………

….statement(s)…..

…………………………

Objects in a Class

Objects resemble real-world entities and are instances of a class. A single class can have many objects. These objects can access the attributes of a class by using the dot (.) operator.

The 'Self' Keyword

When we declare methods inside a class, the first parameter passed inside every method is the self keyword. The self keyword is used to allow access to the attributes and methods of each object. With the help of a self keyword, each object can have its specific attributes and methods. Suppose we declare a method that takes no argument. Still, we must pass the self keyword as an argument explicitly in that method.

The __init__ method

The __init__ method is a special method that works as a class constructor. This method gets invoked automatically as soon as any object of that class gets instantiated. The constructors are used to initialize all the variables associated with an object.

Class Variable and Instance Variable

Those variables that can be shared by all the instances of the class are called class variables. These are public and declared inside the body of the class but are not restricted under any specific functions.

The instance variables are specific to a particular class instance (object) and are generally specified inside particular methods, like the constructor method.

Creating Our First Class

Now that we have discussed all this terminology, let's create an actual class and see all these terms used inside the class.

Suppose that we have a class of cars. Each can have attributes like Name, Color, Size, Company, etc. Also, they can have functionalities like built-in Wi-Fi, seating space, etc. Let's create a class named Cars and make its objects.

```python
class Cars:
    "A class named Cars is created"

    # class attribute
    car_type = '4-wheeler'
    # instance attribute
    def __init__(self, company_name, model, color):
        self.company_name = company_name
        self.model = model
        self.color = color

    def has_wifi(self):
        print('This car has built-in wifi')

    def seating_space(self):
        print('This car can accomodate minimum four persons')
# creating a new object of Cars class and passing the instance attributes
Car1 = Cars('Mahindra','Scorpio', 'Black')

# Accessing class variable/attribute using dot (.) operator
print(Car1.car_type)

# Accessing instance attributes using dot (.) operator
print('Company name of Car1 is: ',Car1.company_name)
print('Model of Car1 is: ',Car1.model)
print('Color of the car is: ',Car1.color)

# Accessing class member functions using dot (.) operator
Car1.has_wifi()

Car1.seating_space()
```

In the above-written program, we have first declared the name of the class as Cars. Then we create a class attribute/variable named car_type that is declared publically so that it can be made available for everyone to access. Later, we create the __init__() method, which acts as a constructor, and we declare the instance variables inside this special function. The value of the instance variables will be accessible to the specific objects instantiated from the class. Also, we have declared a few methods inside the class that can be accessed by the objects of the class.

When we are done declaring the class, we can move out of the indented block. Then we will create an object of that class with the name Car1. While instantiating the Car1 object, we can pass the values of the instance variable inside the method. As soon as the object gets instantiated, the __init__() constructor method automatically gets invoked and the instance variables are initialized using the passed parameters. Later, we can make a call to these class and instance variables using the (.) dot operator. The output of the program is shown below:

```
= RESTART: C:\Users\Saurabh Gupta\AppData\Local\Programs\Python\Python39\if.py
4-wheeler
Company name of Car1 is:  Mahindra
Model of Car1 is:  Scorpio
Color of the car is:  Black
This car has built-in wifi
This car can accomodate minimum four persons
>>> |
```

Inheritance

We have already stated that one of the main objectives of OOP is to enhance code reusability. The concept of inheritance helps us do exactly that.

The idea of inheritance in OOP is in accordance with the principle of inheritance as it exists in the real world. In the real world, a child inherits properties from his/her parents and has similar properties to his/her parents. In addition to properties derived from his/her parents, the child can have some unique properties of his/her own.
The same concept applies to inheritance in OOP. Inheritance can be defined as the ability of one class to derive characteristics from another class. In simpler terms, inheritance helps us to define a new class (derived class) from a pre-existing class (base class) such that the derived class shares the properties of the base class.

Also, inheritance follows the transitive property. Suppose A is the parent/base class and B is its derived/child class. Then child B can also act as a base class and has its child as class C. We must note that class C will inherit its properties from class B, which already inherited properties from class A. This means that class C will have properties of both class A and class B.

In inheritance, the child class possesses an 'IS A' property with its base class.

Syntax

class base_class:

....

..........body of base class.......

....

class derived_class (base_class):

....

......body of derived class......

....

When we define the child/derived class, we put the name of its parent/base class inside parentheses beside the name of the child class. Suppose that we have a base class named Animal that depicts all the animals present in the universe, and it has two derived classes— Cow and Tiger—that depict all the cows and tigers in the world, respectively. Now, we can say Cow and Tiger both have an 'IS A' relationship with the Animal class because Cow is an animal and Tiger is an animal.

Let's try to understand this concept of inheritance using a simple code.

```python
class Animal:
    def legs(self):
        print("This animal has four legs")
    def tail(self):
        print("This animal has a tail")

# child class Cow inherits the base class Animal
class Cow(Animal):
    def food_type(self):
        print("Cow is herbivores")
    def yield_milk(self):
        print('Cow gives us milk')

# child class Tiger inherits the base class Animal
class Tiger(Animal):
    def food_type(self):
        print("Tiger is carnivores")

# Making an object of cow class
c = Cow()
c.legs()
c.tail()
c.food_type()
c.yield_milk()

print("------------------------------")

# Making an object of Tiger class
t = Tiger()
t.legs()
t.tail()
t.food_type()
```

First, we create a base class named Animal that has two methods, named 'legs' and 'tail'. Then, we create two derived classes from the base class, named Cow and Tiger, as both follow a relationship with the Animal class (as explained above). Both of these derived classes have their methods defined inside their body.

Now that we have declared the derived classes, we can create objects of these classes and start accessing the methods belonging to these classes using the dot (.) notation.

We can notice that although the legs() method and the tail() method are not declared inside the body of both Cow and Tiger classes, objects of both these derived classes can access the methods declared inside the Animal class. This is possible because of the property of inheritance. The derived class objects, apart from accessing their own class methods, can access the methods present inside the base class, as the property was inherited into them by their parent class. The example we read above is related to hierarchical inheritance (one of the types that we will read in the next section).

The output of the above-written code will be as shown below:

```
= RESTART: C:\Users\Saurabh Gupta\AppData\Local\Programs\Python\
This animal has four legs
This animal has a tail
Cow is herbivores
Cow gives us milk
------------------------------
This animal has four legs
This animal has a tail
Tiger is carnivores
>>> |
```

```
= RESTART: C:\Users\Saurabh Gupta\AppData\Local\Programs\Python\
This animal has four legs
This animal has a tail
Cow is herbivores
Cow gives us milk
------------------------------
This animal has four legs
This animal has a tail
Tiger is carnivores
>>>
```

Types of Inheritance

Inheritance, in general, can be of multiple types:

i. Single-level inheritance

When a base class has only one derived class, the inheritance is known as single inheritance. It could be depicted in a figure as:

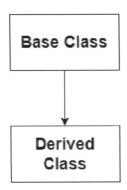

ii. Multi-level inheritance

When a base class has a derived class and that derived class acts as a base class for the next class, this type of inheritance is multi-level inheritance. In such cases, the transitive property of inheritance that we discussed above gets utilized. Pictorially, it could be depicted as:

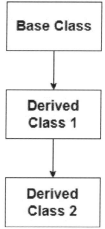

In the above arrangement, Derived Class 1 inherits the property of Base Class, and Derived class 2 inherits the properties of both Base Class and Derived Class 1.

iii. Multiple inheritance

We can even have cases in which a single class has multiple parents such that it derives properties from all these base classes. This type of inheritance is called multiple inheritance. It could be represented as:

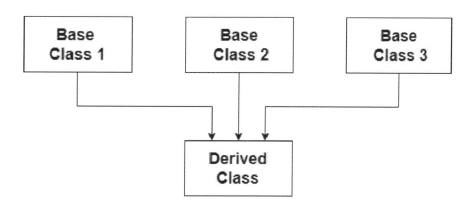

Here, the derived class inherits all the properties from all the base classes 1, 2, and 3.

iv. Hierarchical inheritance

When a single base class can have multiple child/derived classes, it is known as hierarchical inheritance. It could be pictorially represented as:

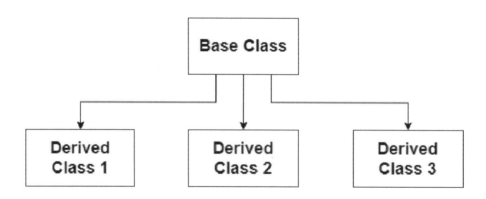

Here, the base class has three derived classes: 1, 2, and 3, respectively. All share the properties defined inside the base class.

An Appeal from the Publisher

Hello wonderful reader!

We hope you are enjoying this book.

We wanted to let you know that you have made an impact on many lives by reading this book.

Just to give you a brief introduction: We are a small publishing company with a team of 8 writers and 2 editors.

Most of our employees come from financially weaker section and our company is the only means they support their families. This is our way of giving back to the society.

We don't have the giant advertising budgets that many other publishers and businesses do online.

So, one way that you can really support our mission and our business is by leaving us a review on this book.

For a small company like us, getting reviews (especially on Amazon) means we can submit our books for advertising.

This means we can actually sell a few copies from time to time and make a bigger impact on the society as a whole. So, every review means a lot to us.

We can't THANK YOU enough for this!

Made in the USA
Middletown, DE
24 October 2021